CHRIST IN GLORY. A panel of the doors of
Santa Sabina, Rome. The carving is of the fifth
century A.D.

# THE CLARENDON BIBLE

Under the general editorship of
BISHOP STRONG, BISHOP WILD, AND
CANON G. H. BOX

# THE EPISTLE

TO THE

# HEBREWS

*In the Revised Version*

WITH INTRODUCTION AND COMMENTARY

BY

## F. D. V. NARBOROUGH, B.D., M.A.

*Formerly Fellow of Worcester College, Oxford*

OXFORD
AT THE CLARENDON PRESS

*Oxford University Press, Amen House, London E.C.4*

EDINBURGH GLASGOW NEW YORK TORONTO MELBOURNE
WELLINGTON BOMBAY CALCUTTA MADRAS CAPE TOWN

*Geoffrey Cumberlege, Publisher to the University*

FIRST PUBLISHED 1930
REPRINTED 1940, 1943, 1946, 1948

PRINTED IN GREAT BRITAIN

# PREFACE

THE problem of the teaching of Holy Scripture at the present time presents many difficulties. There is a large and growing class of persons who feel bound to recognize that the progress of archaeological and critical studies has made it impossible for them to read, and still more to teach, it precisely in the old way. However strongly they may believe in inspiration, they cannot any longer set before their pupils, or take as the basis of their interpretation, the doctrine of the verbal inspiration of the Holy Scripture. It is with the object of meeting the requirements not only of the elder pupils in public schools, their teachers, students in training colleges, and others engaged in education, but also of the clergy, and the growing class of the general public which we believe takes an interest in Biblical studies, that the present series is projected.

The writers will be responsible each for his own contribution only, and their interpretation is based upon the belief that the books of the Bible require to be placed in their historical context, so that, as far as possible, we may recover the sense which they bore when written. Any application of them must rest upon this ground. It is not the writers' intention to set out the latest notions of radical scholars—English or foreign—nor even to describe the exact position at which the discussion of the various problems has arrived. The aim of the series is rather to put forward a constructive view of the books and their teaching, taking into consideration and welcoming results as to which there is a large measure of agreement among scholars.

In regard to form, subjects requiring comprehensive treatment are dealt with in Essays, whether forming part of the introduction or interspersed among the notes. The notes themselves are mainly concerned with the subject-matter of the books and the points of interest (historical, doctrinal, &c.) therein presented ; they deal with the elucidation of words, allusions, and the like only so far as seems necessary to a proper comprehension of the author's meaning.

THOMAS STRONG. ⎫ *General*
HERBERT WILD. ⎬ *Editors.*
GEORGE H. BOX. ⎭

# FOREWORD

THE purpose of this commentary is exegetical, that is to bring out, as far as may be, the meaning of the author of the Epistle to the Hebrews. To enable the Epistle to speak for itself has been the object tenaciously held in view throughout. The scope of the work is thus palpably limited, and lacks largely that element of digressive dissertations to which we have become habituated in commentaries.

Its author wishes to acknowledge gratefully his indebtedness to Dr. Moffatt's Commentary on Hebrews in the International Critical Commentary Series, an indebtedness which is even greater than is indicated by the frequent references to Moffatt which appear in these pages.

F. D. V. N.

# TABLE OF CONTENTS

# LIST OF ILLUSTRATIONS

# INTRODUCTION

## A. THE AUTHORSHIP OF THE EPISTLE

THE authorship of Hebrews has been a much debated question both in ancient and modern times. Pauline authorship seems to have been consistently denied in the Western Church during the second and third centuries. In Alexandria the Epistle was held to be indirectly the work of St. Paul, a letter which he had written in Aramaic and which had been translated by St. Luke,[1] or composed by some friend of St. Paul's from memory of what the apostle had said.[2] From the fourth century, however, the Epistle came to be generally regarded as Pauline, until, with the revival of learning in Europe, doubts were once more expressed by such writers as Erasmus, Luther, and Calvin.

The contents of the letter are such that it is difficult to imagine how the name of St. Paul could ever have become attached to it, except as the result of a rather blind desire to secure such a valuable anonymous work under the aegis of apostolic authority. Though Hebrews shows in rather more than a dozen places signs of the influence of some of the Pauline epistles,[3] its manner of presenting salvation in Christ is, as a whole, entirely different from that of St. Paul. The writer's mind lives in a different world of thought.[4] Indeed the resemblances between our author and St. Paul are surprisingly few, in view of the fact that he was probably a member of the Pauline circle (Heb. 13[23]). 1 Peter is more Pauline than Hebrews, and yet no one would dream of assigning 1 Peter to St. Paul.

The literary style of the letter bears no resemblance to St. Paul's style. Its Greek stands high among New Testament writings, being classical in quality. Nor is any work in the New Testament more carefully arranged than Hebrews. Its argument and style

---

[1] Clement of Alexandria, quoted in Eusebius's *Ecclesiastical Hist.* vi. 14.

[2] Origen quoted in Eusebius, *op. cit.*, vi. 25.

[3] See the list of such passages appended to the present section (p. 18), and notes on these passages in the commentary *ad loc.*

[4] For e.g. the difference between St. Paul and Hebrews in regard to the significance of the Jewish Law, see note on 10[3].

run smoothly on from beginning to end.[1] Points which are to be developed later are indicated beforehand, and references are made back to what has been already established. All this is in the severest contrast to St. Paul's passionate and disorderly method of composition, his habit of digressing without ever recovering the thread of the argument or even completing his sentences.

A single verse in Hebrews puts the question of Pauline authorship finally out of court. In $2^{3f}$ the writer describes the manner in which the Faith of Christ had come both to his readers and to himself:—that which had 'at the first been spoken through the Lord was confirmed unto us by them that heard; God also bearing witness with them, both by signs and wonders'. In view of the circumstances of St. Paul's conversion and of his claim in Gal. $1^{12}$ ('Neither did I receive the Gospel from man, nor was I taught it, but it came to me through revelation of Jesus Christ') it is impossible to believe that he could ever have written Heb. $2^{3f}$. The author of Hebrews was evidently one who, like his readers, had been converted in the ordinary course of evangelization.

A remark of Origen[2] is probably the last word on the subject of the authorship—'Who wrote the Epistle God only knows certainly.' So few of the names of even the leading Christians of the first century have been preserved to us that no attempt to label the letter with one of these extant names will carry conviction unless very strongly supported by the internal evidence. Of the various persons to whose composition the Epistle has at various times been assigned the following are worthy of mention in this connexion, Luke, Barnabas, Priscilla, Silvanus, and Apollos.

*Luke.* The supposed similarity between the literary style of Hebrews and that of the third Gospel and the Acts does not really extend far beyond the approximation of all these writings to classical models and the influence of the LXX upon all three

---

[1] For the one exception which 'proves' this rule see $10^{17}$ with note in Commentary *ad loc.*

[2] Quoted by Eusebius, *op. cit.*, vi. 25.

# The Authorship of the Epistle

alike.[1] Nor does the argument from the universalism and occasional Paulinism of the Epistle carry us very far in conviction of Lucan authorship. The most that can be said in favour of this hypothesis is drawn from a comparison between the Epistle and Stephen's speech in Acts 7, on the supposition that Stephen's words are a free composition by St. Luke. Acts 7 contains a review of early Hebrew history slightly similar to that in Heb. 11, with a similar emphasis on the call of Abraham and on the fact that the patriarch himself possessed no portion of the promised land.[2] Both Acts 7 and the Epistle refer to the fact that the Tabernacle was built after the divine pattern shown to Moses on Mt. Sinai.[3] Finally the Jewish tradition that the Law was given through the ministry of angels appears both in Acts 7[53] and Heb. 2[2], an idea which finds place elsewhere in the New Testament only in Gal. 3[19]. These parallelisms are noteworthy; but Lucan authorship of Hebrews would be a bold and precarious inference to draw from them.[4] 'Author' or 'Pioneer' ($ἀρχηγός$) occurs in Heb. 2[10] and 12[2], and elsewhere in the New Testament only in the earlier sermons in the Acts (3[15] and 5[31]). But the theology and the phraseology of the early speeches in Acts are so distinctive, and so different from those of the Lucan writings as a whole, that scholarship inclines more and more to regard them as representing sources used by St. Luke rather than as his own compositions.

*Barnabas.* Tertullian[5] mentions an epistle to the Hebrews by Barnabas, and this is more likely to be a reference to our Epistle than to the fantastic ultra-Alexandrian 'Epistle of Barnabas'. But apart from the fact that the argument of Hebrews centres largely round the 'Levitical' system there seems to be little to support this solitary ascription of the Epistle to Barnabas, the Levite of Cyprus.[6]

*Priscilla.* Harnack[7] has suggested that the Epistle was the

---

[1] Westcott (*Comment.*, p. xlviii) gives a list of the more striking words or phrases common to Hebrews and the Lucan writings. His list numbers nineteen.
[2] Acts 7[5], and Heb. 11[9] (see note).　　　　[3] Acts 7[44], and Heb. 8[5].
[4] For a positive argument against Lucan authorship see note on 10[20].
[5] *De Pudicitia*, 20.　　　　[6] Acts 4[36].
[7] Harnack, *Z.N.T.W.*, 1900, S. 16–41.

work of Priscilla, aided perhaps by her husband Aquila. He considers that, in view of the Pauline prejudice against any prominence of women in the Church, the theory of Priscilla's authorship
would account for the anonymous state in which Hebrews has
come down to us and the absence from this epistle of the opening
paragraph of greeting, in which it was the custom of the writer
of a letter to give his name. The hypothesis would explain also,
so Harnack states, the prominence of women among the heroes
of faith in Heb. 11. But women do not, as a matter of fact,
occupy a striking position in that chapter. Nor would it accord
with the evidence of the New Testament as a whole to suppose
an epistle so authoritative in tone as Hebrews to be the work of
a woman.

*Silvanus*, 'through whom' 1 Peter was written (1 Peter 5$^{12}$),
has been suggested as the author of Hebrews in view of resemblances between Hebrews and 1 Peter. The most striking similarities noticed are here given and are not noted in the commentary.
It will be seen that they are extensive enough to suggest some
literary connexion between the epistles,[1] an influence of one
author upon the other. In view of the uncertainty of the extent
of Silvanus's connexion with 1 Peter [2] and of the scantiness of our
information about him (even if he be identical with the Silas of
the Acts) the hypothesis of his authorship of Hebrews is too
purely conjectural to deserve serious consideration.

*Antitype* is used in a similar way in Heb. 9$^{24}$ ('like in pattern'
R.V.) and 1 Pet. 3$^{21}$.

*Pilgrim* (Gr. παρεπίδημος) is a term applied to the faithful soul
in Heb. 11$^{13}$ and 1 Pet. 1$^{1}$ and 2$^{11}$.

'*The house*' or '*household of God*', as a description of the Church,
appears in Heb. 3$^{6}$, 10$^{21}$, and 1 Pet. 2$^{5}$, 4$^{17}$.

'*Living word*' is found, though in rather different senses, in
Heb. 4$^{12}$, and 1 Pet. 1$^{23}$.

---

[1] The present writer, inclining to the belief that 1 Peter is the work of
St. Peter (who perished in the Neronian persecution), therefore supposes
that 1 Peter has influenced the writer of Hebrews, and not vice versa.

[2] 'Through Silvanus' may mean merely that he was the author's
amanuensis.

A literary work by a Christian convert of the first century A.D. Part of a translation of the Old Testament from Hebrew into Greek. (The MS. illustrated is a palimpsest, a work in Hebrew having been written over the Greek.)

'*To inherit a blessing*' (εὐλογίαν κληρονομῆσαι) in Heb. 12²⁷ and 1 Pet. 3⁹.

*Christ as the Shepherd* in Heb. 13²⁰ and 1 Pet. 2²⁵, but so also, of course, in John 10¹¹ᶠᶠ.

*To bear sins* (ἀνενεγκεῖν ἁμαρτίας) in Heb. 9²⁸ and 1 Pet. 2²⁴.

*Sprinkling* in Heb. 12²⁴ and 1 Pet. 1². *Once* (of Christ's suffering for sins) in Heb. 9²⁸ &c., and 1 Pet. 3¹⁸, but cf. also Rom. 6¹⁰.

*Spotless* (ἄμωμος) (of Christ's offering) in Heb. 9¹⁴ and 1 Pet. 1¹⁹.

With 'reproached for the name of Christ' in 1 Pet. 4¹⁴ compare the 'reproach of Christ' in Heb. 11²⁶ and 13¹³.

Notice how both writers describe their respective epistles as 'brief exhortations', 1 Pet. 5¹² and Heb. 13²².

Note the very similar doxologies in 1 Pet. 4¹¹ and Heb. 13²¹, and the similarities of the concluding prayers in 1 Pet. 5¹⁰ and Heb. 13²¹.

Except where it is otherwise noted, the above parallelisms between Hebrews and 1 Peter are unparalleled in the rest of the New Testament.

*Apollos.* Martin Luther's guess that the Epistle was the work of Apollos is at least as probable as any other theory of authorship. According to Acts 18²⁴ Apollos was an Alexandrian Jew, 'mighty in the Scriptures',[1] and the author of Hebrews stands out even among New Testament writers as mighty in the Scriptures of the Old Testament, upon his detailed knowledge of which nearly the whole of his argument is based. The Alexandrian affinities [2] of the author will appear in the course of the commentary, to some extent in his occasional use of the Book of the Wisdom of Solomon,[3] but beyond question in his close acquaintance with the writings of the great Alexandrian Philo.[4] The Epistle *as a whole* resembles, too, such Alexandrian products as the work of Philo or the Epistle of Barnabas, in its general presentation of the details of the Old Covenant as symbolizing deeper spiritual realities than appeared on their surface. If

---

[1] It is probably needless to remark that a reference in the New Testament to 'the Scriptures' means the Jewish Scriptures.

[2] On Alexandrianism see 'General Note on Philo and the Alexandrians', pp. 17 ff.            [3] See notes on 1³, 2¹⁴, 4¹², 12¹⁷.

[4] e.g. notes on 3⁴, 4¹², 5¹²⁻¹⁴, 6¹³, ¹⁸, 11⁴, 13⁵.

Apollos was the author a puzzling phenomenon in $6^2$ becomes at once intelligible. Why does that verse include 'baptisms', in the plural, among the first elements of Christian instruction? Apollos (Acts $18^{25}$) knew the baptism of John before he was brought to the baptism of Jesus.

Further, the epithet λόγιος is applied to Apollos in Acts $18^{24}$, meaning either that he was 'learned' or 'eloquent', but rather more probably the latter. There is much in Hebrews to suggest that its author was an orator. He writes at times as if he were haranguing his readers ($2^5$, $6^9$), a tendency specially marked in $11^{32}$, where he uses the phrase 'the time will fail me if I tell' (Gr. ἐπιλείψει με γὰρ διηγούμενον ὁ χρόνος) which is paralleled in Demosthenes, *de Corona*, 324 (ἐπιλείψει με λέγονθ᾽ ἡ ἡμέρα) and elsewhere. Another regular rhetorical phrase appears in $8^1$, translated in the R.V. 'Now in the things which we have been saying the chief point is . . .' (Gr. κεφάλαιον δὲ ἐπὶ τοῖς λεγομένοις). Cicero (*ad Attic*. v. 18) uses the Greek word κεφάλαιον, showing how technical a term it had become for the consummation of an argument. A recent writer on Hebrews goes so far as to remark,[1] 'Perhaps we might best explain it as the work of an eloquent teacher who was separated from his church and wrote a discourse for some one else to deliver in his name.' Certainly the author himself describes his letter ($13^{22}$) as a 'word of exhortation'. And Dr. Moffatt fills several pages of introduction to his commentary[2] with various illustrations of the rhetorical tendencies of our writer, among which we may note the following: (*a*) The Epistle reproduces the conventional rhythmical cadences popularized by the orator Isocrates. (*b*) The author occasionally uses a not quite natural word for the sake of its *assonance* with other words in the sentence.[3] (*c*) That he has a partiality for alliteration.[4] (*d*) That he uses (in $6^8$) a rather unexpected phrase 'nigh unto cursing' which is found in the orator Aristides (*Orat. in Rom.* 370).

[1] *The Epistle to the Hebrews*, by E. F. Scott (T. & T. Clark, 1922), p. 9.
[2] In the International Critical Commentary Series (T. & T. Clark, 1924), pp. lvi ff.
[3] e.g. μετέσχηκεν for assonance with προσέσχηκεν, in $7^{13}$.
[4] See the remarkable alliteration in the Greek of $11^{28}$.

If the above considerations have not established the authorship of Apollos, they will at least have shown the plausibility of Luther's conjecture, and have called attention to some interesting characteristics of the Epistle.

### General Note on the Pauline Epistles and Hebrews.

A list of similarities between verses of Hebrews and passages from St. Paul's epistles. Those marked with an asterisk are definite enough to suggest that the author of Hebrews was consciously influenced by knowledge of the Pauline sentence in question.

In each case reference should be made to note in the commentary *ad loc.*

| | | |
|---|---|---|
| Rom. $8^{29}$ | cf. Heb. | $1^6$ (the first-born). |
| *1 Cor. $12^{11}$ | ,,    ,, | $2^4$ (according to his will). |
| Rom. $11^{36}$ | ,,    ,, | $2^{10}$ (for whom are all things and through whom are all things). |
| Rom. $15^{16 \, f.}$ | ,,    ,, | $5^1$ (in things pertaining to God). |
| Rom. $5^{19}$ and ⎱ *Phil. $2^8$ ⎰ | ,,    ,, | $5^8$ (the obedience of Christ through suffering). |
| Rom. $15^{25}$ | ,,    ,, | $6^{10}$ (ministering to the saints). |
| Rom. $8^{34}$ | ,,    ,, | $7^{25}$ (Christ's intercession). |
| Rom. $6^{10}$ | ,,    ,, | $7^{27}$ and $9^{28}$ (see note). |
| Gal. $3^{19}$ (cf. ⎱ 1 Tim. $2^5$) ⎰ | ,,    ,, | $8^6$, $9^{15}$, $12^{24}$ (Christ the mediator of the Covenant). |
| Col. $1^{15}$ and ⎱ *Col. $2^{17}$ ⎰ | ,,    ,, | $10^1$. |
| Rom. $12^{19}$ | ,,    ,, | $10^{30}$. |
| *Rom. $1^{20}$ | ,,    ,, | $11^3$. |
| *Rom. $4^{19}$ | ,,    ,, | $11^{12}$. |
| *2 Cor. $4^{18}$ | ,,    ,, | whole of chapter 11 and $12^2$. |
| Gal. $4^{26 \, f.}$ | ,,    ,, | $12^{22}$. |

Study of the above list, with reference to notes in the commentary, will establish the influence of Romans, 1 and 2 Corinthians, Colossians, and Philippians upon the author of Hebrews. The influence of Romans is particularly marked, and Hebrews was probably written from Italy, see Introd., p. 27.

*General Note on Philo and the Alexandrians.*

Philo was a contemporary of our Lord, a prominent member of the large Jewish community in Alexandria. While our Lord was teaching and working in Palestine, Philo, in Egypt, was writing books in which the tendency to combine Jewish piety with Greek philosophy reaches its fullest development. The Jews

The harbour of Alexandria to-day

of Alexandria, living in close contact with Greek culture, and far from the ceremonial of the Temple and the influences of the strict and narrow teaching of the scribes of Jerusalem, were absorbing the atmosphere of the Platonism, which was a dominant school of thought in their immediate neighbourhood. In the Wisdom of Solomon,[1] for example, the first ten chapters of which are usually dated shortly before the beginning of the Christian era, the un-Jewish, Platonistic doctrine of the pre-existence of the soul appears in $8^{19 f}$, as well as a Platonistic 'depreciation of the body'

[1] For the affinities between 'Wisdom' and 'Hebrews', see p. 14.

in $9^{15}$. Philo goes much further, inasmuch as, by way of apology for Judaism to his contemporaries and neighbours, he definitely sets out to show that the Jewish Faith is intellectually respectable and possesses close affinities with the conclusions of the Greek philosophers. In this enterprise Philo was driven, not unnaturally, to the constant expedient of allegorization. The use of the allegorical method of interpretation of a written text was not of course confined to Alexandria. It has its origin in simple realization of the fact that no great literature will yield its richest treasures to cursory and prosaic study. But the search for deeper meanings hidden beneath the surface of a text rapidly becomes an absorbing and misleading occupation unless the imagination is sternly disciplined by the reason. Allegorization may have a variety of motives. Certain sophists, for instance, are well known to have used the allegorical method in order to render presentable to a more refined age the cruder parts of Homer. Jewish rabbis, 'toiling at the sacred text' of the Old Testament, eager to bring out of that treasure-house things new as well as old, searched for concealed significance behind the plain sense of the narrative.[1] Philo is driven to extremes in this respect by virtue of the inherent difficulty of his task of squaring the Old Testament with the best of pagan philosophy. Nevertheless he was far from regarding the method as a necessary *evil*. He conceived it to be a religious duty, comparable to the rite of initiation into the Greek mystery religions. In this idea he was encouraged by his own particular (Greek rather than Jewish) theory of inspiration. The prophet was to him one temporarily deprived of the use of his own senses, and entirely controlled by the divine afflatus. In such a condition he uttered mysteries deeper than he himself understood. Of the occult significance of these mysteries Philo regarded it as his duty to be the exponent. Of the allegorizing tendency, which is so marked a characteristic of Philo, we find a striking instance in the view of Melchizedek adopted in Heb. 7 ; [2] in the interpretation of promised rest (in $4^3$) and of the oath to Abraham (in $6^{17}$), as well as in the discussion of the faith of Abel,

[1] A typical piece of Rabbinic allegorization is to be found in Gal. $4^{21\text{-}31}$.
[2] See notes *ad loc.*, especially on $7^3$.

Enoch, Noah, and Jacob in chap. 11.[1] A further point of contact between Alexandrian thought, as represented by Philo, and the Epistle to the Hebrews is closely connected with this method, or principle, of allegorization. Philo is as un-Jewish as he is Platonistic in his emphasis of the transcendence of God and his consequent tendency to represent Him as aloof from the Universe.

The Jewish community in Egypt. An Aramaic papyrus from Elephantine, containing evidence of a Jewish temple in Egypt in the fifth century B.C.

Plato had attempted to bridge the gulf between the divine unchangeableness and purity of being on the one hand and the material world on the other by his doctrine of Ideas, which are, briefly and roughly speaking, the thoughts of God, apprehended by us through the medium of particular phenomena. Along this line of thought, which was adopted by Philo, the material universe is approached as sacramental, as consisting of earthly manifestations or expressions of heavenly realities. And this

[1] See notes *ad loc.*

enthusiasm for the inward behind the outward is not only a great stimulus to the employment of the allegorical method, but also consonant with the peculiar treatment in 'Hebrews' of the Jewish Law and cultus as 'copies' or 'shadows' of a greater Reality.[1]

Of the Ideas or Powers of God in Philo, those activities of the mind of God which give form to the phenomena of the Universe, the foremost is designated by him the Logos. Of Logos both 'Reason' and 'Word' are inadequate translations, inasmuch as it includes both ideas. The Philonic Logos is the archetypal Idea of the whole process of creation in which all other divine Ideas are included and held together. The Logos is indeed Philo's mode of picturing the Immanence of God, and is closely parallel both to the Platonic conception of the divine Nous and to the personification of Wisdom in the Jewish Wisdom-literature.[2] The influence of Philo's Logos-doctrine upon the orthodox conception of the Person of Christ is well known. The Epistle to the Hebrews, unlike the Fourth Gospel, nowhere explicitly applies to Christ the name of Logos,[3] but we may reasonably suppose, in view of the writer's acquaintance with the works of Philo, that the doctrine of the Logos assisted him to his conception of the cosmic and creative significance of the Eternal Son of God.[4] Philo, it may be added, had no conception of the Logos as a Person. It was in Christian theology, through identification with Christ, that the Logos was personalized.

## B.  THE DESTINATION AND PURPOSE OF THE EPISTLE

The earliest appearance of the title 'To Hebrews' is in Tertullian,[5] at the beginning of the third century. It is a strangely and suspiciously vague title, which would suggest, if taken seriously, that the destination of the Epistle was the Hebrew world at

[1] See $8^{5\,f}$, $9^{25}$, $10^1$ with notes *ad loc.*
[2] e.g. in Prov. 8.
[3] See note on $4^{12}$.
[4] See note on $1^2$.
[5] *De Pudicitia*, 20.  No doubt he is referring to our Epistle, though he specifies Barnabas as the author.

large, or Jewish Christians generally, or at the least all those Jewish Christians who spoke Aramaic.[1]

The contents of the letter, on the contrary, leave no room for doubt that it was addressed to some particular local Christian community,[2] which the title entirely fails to locate. ' To Hebrews ' may well represent merely a vague attempt to find an appropriate title for an unnamed epistle, on the part of some one, in the second century, who was impressed by the prominence in its pages of arguments from the Old Testament. Nevertheless, the majority of scholars have accepted the title as correctly describing the recipients as Jewish Christians, and have suggested various suitable motives for the writing of such an epistle to such a community. Some have supposed that it was written in order to reconcile Jewish Christians, who had remained in some degree attached to Judaism, to the destruction of Jerusalem in A.D. 70, by showing them how all that had been of value in Judaism was to be found in the Christian Church. Others have suggested that it was written before the actual fall of Jerusalem, in preparation for that event, at a moment when Jewish Christians in Palestine were being eagerly canvassed by Jews who claimed their aid against the Romans on the ground of patriotism. Others again have assumed, more simply, that the motive of the Epistle was to prevent some Jewish Christians from relapsing into Judaism, when their first enthusiasm for the Christian Faith had begun to flag.[3]

None of these different Judaistic theories seems to be easily tenable in view of 13[9], where, referring directly to the dangers which beset his readers, the author exhorts them not to be ' carried away by divers and strange teachings: for it is good that the heart be stablished by grace; not by meats, wherein they that occupied themselves were not profited'. It is difficult to believe that if the problem in question had been the connexion between the readers of the Epistle and ordinary Judaism, it would have been referred to as ' divers and strange teachings '. Nor could it

[1] Aramaic-speaking Jews is the meaning of ' Hebrews ' in Acts 6[1], and probably in Phil. 3[5].                    [2] See e.g. 13[7, 23, 24].
[3] For these theories see further, section on the date of the Epistle, pp. 29 ff.

be said that 'the establishing of the heart by meats' would be a natural phrase to use as a summary of the essence of Judaism. At this point we are faced with a momentary dilemma; for if we deny the existence of any anti-Judaistic motive in the epistle we render meaningless one of the main features of its argument—the abrogation and supersession of Judaism. A markedly Jewish tendency, which could, however, be naturally described as 'divers and strange teachings' and as a doctrine of 'meats', is the hypothesis for which we are in search as calculated to cover the facts of this epistle.

A comparison between St. Paul's Epistle to the Colossians [1] and the Epistle to the Hebrews yields some remarkable results. In Colossians $2^{20f}$ St. Paul quotes the precepts of an asceticism which forbade the consumption of certain kinds of food—'handle not, nor taste'; and in $2^{16}$ he exhorts the Colossians not to put food regulations in the forefront of their religion, 'Let no man judge you in meat or drink'. Further, the false teachers at Colosse were not only ascetic but Judaistic.[2] They urged the importance not only of meats but of the observance of new moon and Sabbath (Col. $2^{16}$). In fact, St. Paul was confronted at Colosse by a Jewish variety of Gnosticism, such as characterized the Essenes, and in which Christian ingredients were intermixed as well.

The Gnosticism which abounded in the first centuries of the Christian era was not so much a particular religion as a general tendency. There was an almost endless variety of Gnostic systems, eclectic, syncretistic, in some of which were strains both of Judaism and Christianity. But all systems of Gnosticism started alike from the same common ground—a belief that matter was in itself evil. This was their solution, if such it may be called, of the problem of evil. Upon this fundamental axiom two corollaries followed: (1) that the material world, being evil, could not be the creation of the good God. Accordingly most of the Gnostics postulated a series of Gnostic emanations out of the Godhead, a kind of genealogical line of heavenly beings, until there appeared

---

[1] Known to the author of Hebrews. See p. 16.
[2] For the nature of the Colossian heresy see Lightfoot's *Commentary*.

heavenly beings far enough removed from the ultimate God, stupid enough or debased enough, to create the physical universe. With these aeons man, in his relation to the divine, had to reckon, for they inhabited and controlled the different heavens; and salvation consisted partly in knowing their names, and thus possessing passwords, which would secure entrance to the heavens. In the *Jewish* Gnostic systems these heavenly beings were identified with the angels of Judaism. Thus the worship of angels is condemned by St. Paul in connexion with the Jewish Gnostics of Colosse (Col. $2^{18}$), as it is deprecated in the Book of Revelation (Rev. $22^{8\,f}$).

The second corollary of the Gnostic axiom, that matter is evil, is in the sphere not of faith but of morals. Most of the Gnostics, such as the Essenes, led an ascetic life, abstaining from marriage and animal food and indulging in constant washings to free themselves from the contaminations of matter.[1] But, inasmuch as the complete avoidance of matter is for a physical being a rather hopeless task, some of the Gnostics took a different line. As they could not avoid matter, they would develop the utmost contempt for it. What a man did with his body was a question to which the enlightened would feel complete indifference. Thus did Gnostics take in practice divergent paths, some towards an exaggerated asceticism, others towards immorality. Gnostics of the latter type are referred to as 'teaching fornication', in Rev. $2^{14,\ 20-22}$.

From what has already been said it will be clear that Gnosticism in which there was a blend of Christianity must have been a very different religion from the orthodox Christian faith. In fact, Gnosticism merely adopted Christ as one of its aeons or angels, and refused, consistently with its proclamation of matter as inherently evil, to affirm any real Incarnation, any assumption of 'flesh and blood' by Christ. He could only have *seemed* to possess a body.

The hypothesis that Hebrews was written in opposition to a Jewish type of Gnosticism, similar to that which was vexing

[1] For the washings of the Essenes (Jewish Gnostics) see Josephus, *B.J.*, II. viii. 5.

the Colossian Christians, throws a flood of light on the contents of the Epistle. The anti-Judaistic 'motif' of the Epistle remains entirely relevant. The reference to 'divers and strange teachings' and a doctrine of salvation by 'meats', in $13^9$, becomes perfectly natural, as does the similar reference, in $9^{10}$, to 'meats and drinks and divers washings'.[1] We enter, in the light of this hypothesis, upon a new understanding of the author's lengthy exposition of the superiority of Christ to angels. We may admit that this exposition has also the further purpose of establishing the superiority of Christianity to the Jewish Law, inasmuch as the Law was 'spoken through angels' ($2^2$). We may admit also that the superiority of Christ to angels is only one of a series of demonstrations in the epistle of His absolute superiority, and that it is followed by a demonstration of His superiority to Moses. But while the former demonstration is the opening theme of the epistle and occupies nearly two chapters, the latter is contained within the compass of five verses ($3^{2-6}$), a strange fact if the objective of the epistle was Judaism proper, of which Moses was the representative figure.

In the light of the Jewish-Gnostic hypothesis as to the purpose of the Epistle we can understand the author's statement, in $2^5$, that heaven is not subjected to the control of angels, and his emphatic denial, in $2^{16}$, of any idea that Christ's nature was that of an angel, as well as his insistence, in $2^{14}$, on the fact that Christ took flesh and blood. The author's rigorism too becomes intelligible [2] if he was combating a Gnostic apostasy which might as easily land its devotees in immorality as in asceticism. His laudation, in $13^4$, of the honourableness of continent marriage would be highly significant as a double-edged thrust alike at the immoral and at the ascetic type of Gnostic. It would certainly not have been necessary to emphasize the sanctity of marriage to the orthodox Jew or to Christians who were falling under his influence.

A difficulty in the way of the Jewish-Gnostic hypothesis must now be faced. Gnostic Judaism, consistently with its attitude

---

[1] See, further, note in Commentary on $9^{10}$.
[2] See Introd., Section D (e), pp. 45–47, for a full treatment of the author's 'rigorism'.

towards material things, renounced all participation in the Temple sacrifices. It is true that no evidence of this fact is forthcoming from the Epistle to the Colossians, but St. Paul has no occasion in that letter to allude to Jewish sacrifices; and the fact is established beyond doubt in that classical instance of Jewish Gnosticism, Essenism.[1]

At first sight such a consideration might appear fatal to the theory that Gnostic Judaism was the heresy combated in an epistle which argues so largely from the Jewish sacrificial system.

Further reflection removes the difficulty. The position of Jewish Gnostics was fundamentally illogical in this very respect. Belief that matter was essentially evil was irreconcilable with what the Law enjoined. Judaism and Gnosticism were really incompatible. Further, the Essenes, we are told, so venerated Moses (the law-giver) as to punish with death any of their members who blasphemed his name,[2] and the very passage in Josephus [3] which tells us that the Essenes took no part in the sacrifices, the performance of which was the main purpose of the existence of the Temple, states also that they sent gifts to the Temple. In fact Jewish Gnostics were faced with a dilemma, one horn of which was their contempt of material things, and the other the fact that their Law enjoined, as the mode of approaching God, the offering of material things. In regard to the sacrificial system they knew not where they stood.

Of this sacrificial system the author of Hebrews undertakes to show the real inwardness. He will have nothing to do with any theory of flesh and blood as inherently evil. Indeed he emphasizes the fact that flesh and blood were assumed by Christ.[4] Moreover, he points out that the Law itself, so far from depreciating the value of material things, represents remission of sins as dependent upon the shedding of blood.[5] At this point he lays his finger on the fundamental anomaly of the heresy which he has in view. On the other hand he admits the inefficacy of 'the blood of bulls and goats'.[6] It was, in fact, as limited in significance and value as other 'carnal ordinances' such as 'meats, drinks and

---

[1] Josephus, *Antiq.*, xviii. 1, 5.                [2] Josephus, *B. J.*, II. viii. 9.
[3] *Antiq.*, xviii. 1. 5.            [4] $2^{14}$.          [5] $9^{22}$.          [6] $10^4$.

divers washings'[1] which loomed large in the Jewish Gnostic system.[2] Its function was no more than to be a 'parable'[3] of the spiritual offering of Christ,[4] the essence of which, though it expressed itself in blood shedding, was the dedication of His will to God.[5]

Judaism and Christianity alike, the author would say, forbid us to condemn the material as essential evil. 'I undertake to show you that the material has a true place in the divine harmony. I admit, however, that it is a subordinate place. The physical is the shadow, or at best the image[6] of a greater, immaterial, spiritual reality.' The Platonistic tone of the philosophy of this epistle[7] is in fact an attempt to set the physical world in its proper perspective in the eyes of Gnostics.

If a tendency to Gnosticism was the danger besetting the recipients of the Epistle, its destination was probably some church in Asia Minor, where the church of Colosse was situated and where Gnosticism had its native home. Against such a location there is no real argument in favour of Palestine or for believing that its recipients had been born Jews. To the converted Gentile, just as much as to the Jews, the Old Testament constituted the Holy Scriptures, 'the oracles of God' as St. Paul calls them in writing to the capital of the Gentile world (Rom. 3[2]). Argument from them would be as valid and as impressive to the Gentile as to the Jewish Christian, and would be the obvious line to take against a heresy containing a strong element of Judaism. Nor is it likely that the author of the Epistle was himself a Palestinian Jew. The excellence of his Greek style, and the fact that he never quotes from the Hebrew but always from the Greek Old Testament,[8] suggest rather that he was a very definitely Hellenized Jew of the Dispersion. Nowhere in his letter does he show any knowledge of Hebrew, except that he knows that the

[1] 9[9] f.
[2] For the meats and washings of Essenism see Josephus, *B. J.*, II. viii. 5.
[3] 9[9].    [4] 9[14].    [5] 10[4-10] and notes.
[6] See 10[1] and note *ad loc.*
[7] For the Platonism of Hebrews see pp. 20 and 40 ff.
[8] Heb. 10[30] is an exception to this rule; but neither is it a quotation from the Hebrew. See Commentary, note *ad loc.* For other *apparent* exceptions to this rule see notes on 12[17] and 12[26].

Hebrew names Melchizedek and Salem were interpreted as meaning respectively 'King of righteousness', and 'peace'. But this information might easily have been gained by a Gentile convert to Christianity.

There is nothing, then, in the Epistle which attaches either the writer or the readers of the Epistle to Palestine, while the nature of the heresy rather indicates some district of Asia Minor. If Apollos was the author, Ephesus would have claims for serious consideration. There, according to Acts 18²⁴, Apollos had laboured. He seems to have been there again with St. Paul at or near the time when St. Paul was writing 1 Corinthians[1] (1 Cor. 16¹²). Further, Timothy in whom the recipients of Hebrews were interested (Heb. 13²³) was connected with Ephesus,[2] and the first epistle to Timothy, whether Pauline or not, tells us of the presence at Ephesus of Gnostic teachers who forbade marriage and taught a doctrine of meats (1 Tim. 4³).

The theory of Rome (probably a house-church in Rome) as the destination of Hebrews has found advocates,[3] and it is certain from 13²⁴ ('They of Italy salute you') that the Epistle was written either to or from some church in Italy. 'They of Italy' (οἱ ἀπὸ τῆς 'Ιταλίας) may signify either 'the inhabitants of Italy where I am writing' or 'such Italian compatriots of yours as are with me where I am'. At first sight this latter interpretation might seem to be required, for Italy is a large area from which to send greetings. The phrase would be natural, however, in the former sense, if the author was writing from some small and obscure Italian town; and Italy does not seem a likely destination for the Epistle, if we are to take 2³ᶠ at all seriously. To Rome at any rate the Gospel probably drifted in the first place in the course of trade and ordinary intercourse,[4] whereas the recipients of this epistle had been definitely and deliberately evangelized by eye-witnesses of Christ, to the accompaniment of apostolic miracles.

[1] For the fact that 1 Corinthians was written at Ephesus see 1 Cor. 16⁸.
[2] Witness the epistles to Timothy.
[3] So e.g. E. F. Scott, *The Epistle to the Hebrews*.
[4] See e.g. Sanday and Headlam, *Romans* (International Critical Commentary), pp. xxv–xxxi.

## · C. DATE OF THE EPISTLE

The question of the date of Hebrews remains as problematical as that of its authorship. It cannot be dated later than A.D. 96, the year in which Clement of Rome wrote to the Corinthians an epistle the language of which is often strongly reminiscent of Hebrews; nor can it be earlier than the Pauline epistles, which have influenced in places its thought and phraseology.[1] But for the determination of a date within these limits—c. A.D. 60 to c. A.D. 90—the internal evidence of the Epistle gives little definite help.

We have no other evidence for a captivity of Timothy to which, perhaps,[2] reference is made in $13^{23}$, nor do we know how long Timothy lived. Scholars have inferred from $2^3$ that the recipients 'belonged to the second generation of Christians'. The 'second generation of Christians' is a very vague term; but the verse in question seems simply to state that the writer and his readers had been converted by eye-witnesses of Christ. $5^{12}$, again, is supposed by some to suggest that a considerable time had elapsed since the foundation of the community to which the letter was sent. In reality the language of the verse is such as an eager Christian leader might address to those whose adherence to the Christian Faith had been a matter of a few years only. In $10^{32}$ is a reference to a past persecution of the church, but the words 'after ye were en-lightened' suggest that this persecution had followed quickly upon the foundation of the community to which the Epistle was addressed. The exhortation, in $13^7$, to 'remember them that had the rule over you', certainly implies that the original officials of the church were dead. But the verse continues 'considering the issue' (Gr. τὴν ἔκβασιν) 'of their life, imitate their faith', words which seem to suggest death by martyrdom rather than of old age.[3] It is true that the whole tenor of the Epistle suggests that the first Christian enthusiasm of the readers had waned, but this might have happened, especially under the influence of an in-sidious heresy,[4] even before A.D. 60.

---

[1] See p. 16.    [2] See Commentary, note *ad loc.*
[3] But see note in Commentary *ad loc.*
[4] See the preceding Section (B).

We are driven back on the question of the relation of the Epistle to the Fall of Jerusalem in A. D. 70. Consideration of the purpose and destination of the Epistle [1] has led us to deny that its composition had any direct and immediate relation to that event, but we are not therefore precluded from looking for reference to the destruction of the Jewish cultus in an epistle which seeks to prove to Judaisers the complete abrogation of Judaism. Indeed the contents of 'Hebrews' suggest that at the time of writing the Fall of Jerusalem was either known to be impending or accomplished. Such an hypothesis is not demanded by but would give additional significance to 11[10],—Abraham 'looked for a city having the foundations', and to 13[13 f., 2] where the readers are exhorted to a clean breach with Judaism on the ground that they, unlike the Jews, expect no 'abiding city' on earth. Again, in 8[13], the author of Hebrews is bold to say that the Old Covenant was 'nigh unto vanishing' even in Jeremiah's day, while in 9[8] he implies that the first Tabernacle (his symbol throughout the Epistle for the Jewish cultus) no longer 'had standing' (Greek ἐχούσης στάσιν). We must be careful not to draw unnecessary inferences from these two verses. It is possible that neither may mean more than that Judaism has been superseded by Christianity. The wording of the second of them is noticeably vague. The writer does not imply in plain Greek that the 'first Tabernacle' had fallen. He may mean no more than that it had lost its status. But, as in the case of the references to the abiding city, his words gain added force if interpreted in relation to the Fall of Jerusalem, the complete destruction of the apparatus of the Jewish cultus. Against such an interpretation the fact that he writes sometimes [3] as if the Temple ceremonial was still in existence counts for nothing. Josephus, writing later than the destruction of the Temple, uses a similar 'historic present',[4] and the author of Hebrews is thinking not so much of what *was done* in the Temple, as of what *is* prescribed in the Law. He writes throughout the Epistle from knowledge of the Pentateuch rather

[1] See the preceding Section (B).
[2] See notes in Commentary *ad loc.*    [3] In 5[1-4], 7[28], 8[3, 5], &c.
[4] e.g. C. *Apionem*, I. 7.—A priest violating the Mosaic regulations 'is forbidden' to officiate at the altars.

than from personal experience of the cultus, of the Tabernacle and not the Temple. The past tenses of $9^{1-10}$ have as little significance for date as the historic presents of other verses. The reference is to what the Law 'enjoined' or 'enjoins'.

On the other hand the significance of $13^{10-16}$ [1] is an exhortation to Christians not to be ashamed of the meagreness of their cultus. This meagreness is not, the author implies, to be allowed to lead them to hanker after the Jewish ceremonialism. Christians have all the essentials of a true worship. Are we obliged to infer, therefore, that the Jewish cultus was still in existence? Such an inference is not forced upon us. The fall of Jerusalem had not that aspect of finality for the Jews of the first century of our era which it wears for us nearly nineteen hundred years after the event. In the mind of the Jews of A. D. 70 to 90 Judaism was still a system with the Temple cultus at its centre.

A date, then, either just before or more probably soon after A. D. 70 seems, though without much definiteness, to suggest itself for the composition of 'Hebrews'.


## D. LEADING IDEAS OF THE EPISTLE

### (a) *The Christology of the Epistle.*

The aim of the author of Hebrews is to show the all-sufficiency of the Christian Faith. Not Judaism itself nor any subtle combination of Judaism and Gnosticism approach anywhere near to the fullness of the revelation and the redemption available in Christ. Accordingly Christ is represented in the Epistle as revealing the true nature both of God and of man. This is the fundamental basis of its Christology. Christ is the pre-existent son of God,[2] the effulgence of His glory, and the very image of His substance.[3] All that He has done represents the mind and will, the purpose of God the Father.[4] Moreover, as the purpose of Christ's life and death was the bringing of many human beings unto glory,[5] it was fitting[6] that the Son of God should 'become in

---

[1] See note in Commentary *ad loc.*
[2] See $1^2$.     [3] See $1^3$.     [4] See e.g. $10^{5-10}$.     [5] See $2^{10}$.
[6] See note on 'it became him' in $2^{10}$, and 'it behoved him' in $2^{17}$.

all things like unto his brethren',[1] the members of the human race. All this was 'fitting' because Christ's life and death constituted a divine activity *on behalf of men*, and had as their aim and object the opening up of a new way of life[2] for men. Christ was the *Pioneer*[3] of our salvation. What He did for us involves not only our acceptance but also our following. Therefore as His purpose was both to work on behalf of men and also to lead men, it was doubly fitting that He should be 'in all things like unto His brethren'. He thus becomes the ideal of our humanity, in other words, its proper representative in the sight of God,[4] and our example. His life and death were distinguished by all those qualities of loyalty to ideals,[5] fortitude in the face of persecution,[6] and the rest which characterize human life at its best and highest. The realization of those ideals He makes possible for us by virtue of the new access to God which is available through Him,[7] as a result of the putting away of sins which He has achieved for us.

The Christology of the Epistle is further elucidated in the following section on 'Priesthood, Sacrifice, and Atonement'.

## (b) *Priesthood, Sacrifice, and Atonement.*

The essence of the idea of priesthood, whether the Jewish Priesthood or the Priesthood of Christ as depicted in Hebrews, is that of mediation between God and man, of representing God to man, and man to God. The priest of a people declares to them the law of God, and performs for them, representatively, certain ceremonies directed towards God on their behalf.[8] An excellent, but little-known, illustration of the former function of the priest in Judaism is to be found in Haggai $2^{10-13}$: the latter function was discharged by the Jewish priesthood in the offering of sacrifices. Of such sacrifices there was in Judaism a considerable variety,

---

[1] $2^{17}$.      [2] $10^{20}$.      [3] $2^{10}$, $12^2$.

[4] This underlies the Epistle's presentation of Christ as our High Priest. See next section.

[5] See e.g. $2^{13}$ and note.      [6] See e.g. $12^2$ and note.

[7] See e.g. $4^{16}$, and the following section of the Introduction.

[8] Such is the meaning of the phrase 'appointed for men in things pertaining to God', in Heb. $5^1$.

into the details of which it is not necessary to enter, inasmuch as the basic idea of all of them alike was the offering to God of some gift [1] such as was believed to be well-pleasing to Him. Not all the Jewish sacrifices were offered for sins. The 'peace-offering' or 'thank-offering', for example, described in Lev. 3 1-17, 7 11-34 was, as it name implies, a sacrifice of thanksgiving. But more and more, after the humiliation and penitence which resulted psychologically from the Babylonian exile and the adversities which continually followed it, those sacrifices which were offered to atone for the sins of their offerers came into prominence in the Jewish sacrificial system. Such were the burnt-offering (Lev. 1 1-17, 6 8-13), and still more clearly the sin-offering (Lev. 4 1-5 13, 6 24-30), and the great national sacrifices of the Day of Atonement (Lev. 16).

For the understanding of the theological significance of these sacrifices for sin the crucial point in the ceremonial is that at which the offerer solemnly lays his hand on the head of the victim which he is offering, e.g. Lev. 4 4, 15. This action has sometimes been falsely interpreted as representing the transference of the guilt of the offerer to the victim. That this was not its significance is shown by the fact that in certain cases the flesh of the victim of the sin-offering was eaten by the priests (Lev. 6 26), an inconceivable proceeding if the guilt of the offerer was imagined to have been transferred to the victim. Such an interpretation is finally ruled out by the ceremonial of the Day of Atonement. In this ceremonial two goats figured, one of which was offered to God in the manner of the sin-offering (Lev. 16 15-19). With the other goat a ceremony was performed, which is obviously the one instance of transference of guilt from the offerers to the victim (Lev. 16 20-22). The high priest is explicitly said to 'put the sins of the people upon the head' of this goat, which was forthwith driven into the wilderness to become the prey of Azazel, an evil spirit (Lev. 16 8-10). Thus in the only case in which sin was believed to be transferred from the offerer to the victim, the victim was appropriately dedicated not to God but to an evil spirit. The laying of the hand on the heads of victims which were offered to God had quite another significance. As Moses laid his

[1] Generally, but not always, an animal. For an exception see Lev. 2 1ff.

hand on Joshua[1] who was to take his place as the leader of the people, so the offerer laid his hand upon the head of his victim to constitute it his substitute in the sight of God. For this was the theology of sacrifice for sins, that sin was so serious a matter in the sight of God as to entail the forfeiting of the life of the sinner, and that the life of the victim was accepted by God in substitution

כי ביום הזה יכפר עליכם

The High Priest and the Scape-goat. The High Priest has the two lots (Leviticus xvi. 8 ff.) for the two goats, one being the Scape-goat and the other the Sacrificial goat. By Aaron stands the 'fit man' (*ib.* 21) to take the scape-goat to the Wilderness and, presumably, the Deputy High Priest. Notice the veil and the cloud; 'the cloud of incense covering the mercy seat' (*ib.* 13). Above are written the words 'For on this day shall He make atonement for you' (*ib.* 30). From Levy's *Form of Prayers for the Day of Atonement* (London, 1807)

for the forfeited life of the offender himself. Such was the nature of the offerings made by the Jewish priesthood in its role of mediation between man and God.

By the time of the Christian era the priest's function of declaring the Law of God to man had lapsed, his place in this respect had been taken by the scribe. Accordingly, though the writer of Hebrews represents Jesus as undertaking this 'mediating'

[1] Num. 27[18 ff].

office, it is as Son [1] and not as priest that He speaks to us on God's behalf. Christ's priesthood in Hebrews consists in that other aspect of mediation—the representation of humanity before God.[2] Nor is this line of argument in the Epistle due merely to a desire on the author's part to force a parallel between the work of Christ and the function of the Jewish priesthood. The perfection of Christ's humanity is, as we have seen,[3] one of his most cherished convictions, the thought of Christ as our Pioneer, our Example and Leader, marking out the road along which we too must travel to God. Christ is the Ideal of our humanity in the sight of God, and, in this spiritual sense, Priest or High Priest of the human race. Therein is the essential point of contact which the author finds between his understanding of the significance of Jesus and the institution of the Jewish priesthood; all else is development of detail.

But the Jewish priesthood represented men to God in the offering of sacrifices; and Jesus also had 'somewhat to offer', the complete dedication of Himself to the will of God.[4] Further, His sacrifice, like theirs, was 'not without blood',[5] His self-dedication being consummated by the offering of His body[6] on the cross.

What effect does the author of Hebrews conceive of Christ's sacrifice as having (a) upon God and (b) upon men?

No word is said to suggest the placating of an angry God, nor is it said that God was propitiated by the death of Christ. In $2^{17}$ we read that Christ 'made propitiation for the sins of the people'. But the translation is misleading. The Greek ($\epsilon i s$ $\tau \grave{o}$ $i \lambda \acute{a} \sigma \kappa \epsilon \sigma \theta a \iota$ $\tau \grave{a} s$ $\acute{a} \mu a \rho \tau \acute{\iota} a s$ $\tau o \hat{v}$ $\lambda a o \hat{v}$) means literally 'to propitiate the sins of the people', a curious turn of phrase which occurs in connexion with the Old Testament sacrifices[7] and by the choice of which the statement that God was propitiated is avoided, attention being directed to the effect of the death of Christ upon our sins.

But does Hebrews represent the death of Christ as being, on

[1] See $1^2$.    [2] See e.g. $5^{1-10}$ with notes.
[3] See above on the Christology of the Epistle, p. 31.
[4] $10^{5-10}$ with notes.    [5] $9^{7, 12}$.    [6] $10^{10}$.    [7] Lev. $16^{16}$.

the analogy of the Old Testament sacrifices, accepted by God as a substitute for our forfeited lives? Nowhere is this explicitly said. The two phrases which approximate most nearly to the idea are in $9^{22}$ and $9^{28}$. $9^{22}$ states that according to the Jewish Law 'apart from shedding of blood there is no remission'. But the statement is one of mere fact and does not raise the question of the reason for the fact. In $9^{28}$ we read that Christ was offered 'to bear the sins of many'. The words are a direct quotation from Isa. $53^{12}$, and one writer may quote the words of another writer because of their familiarity to his readers without necessarily meaning by them exactly what their author meant. Neither the author of Isa. $53^{12}$ nor Hebrews meant by those words that the sufferer bore in the sight of God the guilt of the sins of many.[1] As we have seen, the whole of the Jewish theory of sacrifice is against such an interpretation. The words can only mean then, what Isa. 53, read as a whole, suggests, that He 'bore the sins of many' by taking upon Himself sufferings which were the consequence not of His own sins but of the sins of others. This is a doctrine of vicarious suffering, not (in Hebrews at any rate) of vicarious punishment. The Epistle stresses throughout the voluntariness of Christ's self-oblation, in regard to which He is represented as the offering Priest as well as the Victim. He willingly underwent unmerited suffering; but whatever may be true of other sufferings, the sufferings of the innocent are not *punishments* in any real sense of the term. If Hebrews implies the Old Testament theory of 'substitution', it is in the sense in which any one who suffers because of the sins of another is a 'substitute'. Such vicarious suffering secures remission of sins for the sinner only when it exercises over him a converting influence. We shall misunderstand and misrepresent the theory of Atonement in Hebrews and in the New Testament generally if we base it upon some supposed transaction between Christ and His Father, instead of upon the transforming influence which the preaching of the Cross had been found to exercise upon the lives of those who had become Christians, which was the fact which gave rise to theories of 'Atonement' and which all the theories are but an attempt to explain.

[1] 'Sin' is used in the Old Testament of guilt or of its consequences.

In $9^{12}$ the writer of Hebrews depicts Christ[1] as entering into the presence of God with the offering of His own blood, the 'blood' standing, as it did in Judaism,[2] for the offered life. To God the offering of such a life is supremely acceptable, inasmuch as it represents the perfect accomplishment of His will.[3] And our High Priest 'ever liveth' in the Most Holy Place 'to make intercession for us'.[4] The phrases create difficulties only if we assume an antithesis between the willingness of Christ and the unwillingness of God, an antithesis entirely ruled out in Hebrews by the emphasis laid both on the identity of nature between Father and Son[5] and on the perfection of Christ's co-operation with the divine Will.[6] Read in the light of those pre-suppositions of the Epistle, the efficacy of Christ's 'sacrifice' and His 'intercession' stand for nothing more nor less than the supreme effectiveness of His performance of the will of God.

We must now examine the manner in which the Epistle represents the effect of Christ's life and death upon men. We say 'life and death' because Hebrews shows a firm grasp of the fact that the latter is not intelligible in isolation from the former.

In reading any book of the New Testament it is necessary to remember that the most axiomatic of his beliefs often go entirely unmentioned by its author, because he is writing to supplement instruction already given and received. This is especially clear in the case of Hebrews. At the beginning of chap. 6 the author refuses to discuss anew what he calls the 'first principles of Christ', of which he none the less in passing sketches the outlines. In giving us this summary of what he describes as 'the foundation', he mentions 'repentance from dead works' (i.e. sins[7]), 'faith toward God', 'baptisms and the laying on of hands'. In $6^4$ the process of conversion is further described as 'enlightenment, the tasting of the heavenly gift, partaking of Holy Spirit, tasting the good word of God and the powers of the age to come'. Such is the author's conception of all that becoming a Christian means, the 'outward signs' of baptism and the laying on of hands, and

---

[1] Cf. also $13^{20}$.             [2] See e.g. Lev. $17^{11}$.
[3] $10^{5-10}$ with notes in Commentary.
[4] See $7^{25}$ and $9^{24}$.         [5] $1^{2}$ f.          [6] $10^{5-10}$.
[7] See notes on $6^1$ and $9^{14}$.

THE HIGH PRIEST. The garments are described in Exodus xxviii and xxxix. On the 'forefront of the mitre' is the back of the 'plate of pure gold' (xxviii. 36) bearing the words '[Holiness to the] Lord': the words in square brackets do not appear in the illustration, presumably the artist imagined them to be on the back. From Walton's Polyglot Bible

therewith the reception of instruction,[1] and a gift of Holy Spirit with 'powers' to help the convert to live henceforth 'the life of the world to come', the life which in $5^9$ is described as 'obedience to Christ'. Repentance stands first and foremost in this list as primary, and of Christ's work for us, which in these verses is outlined as a whole, the Epistle to the Hebrews deals only with a part, the part represented by the word 'repentance'. The concentration on this part of the subject is due largely to the author's conception of religion as being primarily the worship or adoration of God.[2] Worship is impossible to those who have a guilty conscience. Thus repentance and the assurance of forgiveness, i.e. in terms borrowed from the sacrificial system, 'the taking away of sins', are the pre-requisite conditions of the religious life.[3] In the spiritual experience of the readers of the Epistle (a) repentance and (b) the assurance of forgiveness had come through the preaching of the Cross, inasmuch as the Cross was the measure (a) of the heinousness of human sin, (b) of the fullness of the love of God. Thus had the death of Christ cleansed their conscience from dead works 'to serve the living God' ($9^{14}$). As Christians they were 'cleansed and had no more conscience of sins' ($10^2$). Christ had made 'purification of sins' ($1^3$). He had 'put away sin by the sacrifice of Himself' ($9^{26}$, cf. $10^{4, 11}$). He had obtained by His death 'eternal redemption' from sin ($9^{12, 15}$). All these phrases would be meaningless indeed apart from the spiritual experience of those for whom they were written, and the saving vision of the Cross of Christ which, though it had grown dim, had been theirs at the time of their conversion and admission into the Church. With repentance and assurance of forgiveness a new boldness of approach to God had become practicable.[4] The death of Christ had 'as touching the conscience made the worshipper perfect', i.e. on the analogy of the usage of these terms in the Epistle, made perfect worshipping possible.[5]

[1] 'Enlightenment' and 'tasting the good word of God'.

[2] This fundamental conception of religion is emphasized repeatedly in the Commentary. See also Introd., pp. 47 f.

[3] Cf. 'As long as a man has a bad conscience he cannot begin to be a good man.' Denney, *The Death of Christ*, p. 189.      [4] $4^{16}$, $10^{19}$.

[5] See $9^{9 f}$ and $10^{14}$, with note on $9^9$ and Introd., p. 48.

The repentance and assurance of forgiveness which flow from the Cross are described in Hebrews not only as the 'cleansing of the conscience', but as the 'sprinkling of the blood' of Christ. The metaphor (for it obviously does not represent a literal truth) is borrowed not from the regular sacrifices of the Levitical system, of which sprinkling of the worshippers with blood was not a feature, but from the particular sacrifice with which Moses inaugurated the old covenant. With this sacrifice the author deals at some length in $9^{18-22}$, and thereafter in the Epistle when he writes of the sacrifice of Christ it is in terms of this sacrifice that he tends to describe it. In $10^{22}$ 'hearts sprinkled from an evil conscience' is reminiscent of the covenant sacrifice, and even more reminiscent are $10^{29}$ 'the blood of the covenant wherewith he was sanctified', $12^{24}$ 'the blood of sprinkling', and $13^{20}$ 'the blood of the eternal covenant'. What meaning is attached in Hebrews to the new covenant made by Christ, and why is it that the author tends to prefer to describe the death of Christ in terms of the covenant-sacrifice rather than in those of the regular sacrifices of the Jewish Law?

The first of these questions is answered in $10^{15-18}$,[1] where Jeremiah's presentation of the features of the New Covenant is expounded as being on God's part a promise of forgiveness of sins. The New Covenant in Hebrews is that forgiveness of sins which, as we have said, alone makes possible a real worshipping relationship between a people and their God. Christ's death is described as the *covenant* sacrifice because it is the means whereby men attain to the repentance and forgiveness, which is the first condition of the covenant-relationship. The covenant-sacrifice of Moses had, for the writer, this additional attraction, that the sprinkling of blood upon the people which accompanied it provided him with an analogy and a metaphor for that effect of Christ's death upon the conscience which is so primary in his thoughts about the Atonement.

A few phrases used in the Epistle in connexion with the 'priestly' death of Christ remain to be examined. In $10^{10, \, 14, \, 29}$ and $13^{12}$ the effect of Christ's death is said to be our 'sanctifica-

[1] See notes *ad loc.*

tion'. This calls for no further discussion in view of its obvious parallelism to the 'cleansing of the conscience' and to the 'sprinkling of the blood'.

In 2[9-15] occur a series of sentences to the effect that Christ tasted death on behalf of (i.e. for the benefit of) every man, that the effect of His death is to deliver us from the fear of death, and that 'through His death He brought to nought him that had the power of death, that is the devil'. Only the last of these phrases calls for comment, the simple comment that, inasmuch as the death of Christ 'takes away' sin, it obviously 'brings to nought the devil'.[1]

It is, perhaps, needless to remark that though the Epistle centres to some extent around the ceremonial of the Day of Atonement as the most solemn form of sin-offering, there is not the slightest suggestion of any parallelism between Christ and the 'scape-goat' (or 'goat for Azazel', the evil spirit) to which on that occasion the guilt of the people was believed to be transferred. In 13[11] Christ is compared to the other victims of the Day of Atonement whose bodies were burned 'outside the camp', and whose blood was offered in the sanctuary, but of the transference of the guilt of the community to whom there was, as we have seen, no thought.

Christ, then, is our High Priest, inasmuch as His self-sacrifice has redeemed us, repentant and forgiven, from our sins. 'Through Him', our Priest, we offer our sacrifices. These (in 13[15]) are described as 'a sacrifice of praise' (Gr. θυσίαν αἰνέσεως), the term applied in Lev. 7[12] to the peace- or thank-offering. The sin-offering having once for all been made, the thank-offering remains for us to offer.

## (c) *The Idealism of the Epistle.*

More must be added [2] by way of introduction to a leading conception of the Epistle which will be illustrated in many of the notes on the text, viz. the 'idealism' of its philosophic outlook. By idealism we mean that system of thought of which Plato is the spiritual father and which views the transitory

---

[1] See also note on 2[14].

[2] In addition to what has been said on pages 19 and 26.

THE HEAVENLY JERUSALEM. A vision of the Temple, from a Domestic Passover Service Book printed at Amsterdam in 1695

phenomena of human experience as expressions of certain eternal spiritual ideas, which constitute ultimate reality. Platonism was in the atmosphere at Alexandria,[1] and, in a rather materialized form, a parallel movement of thought obtained among the writers of Jewish Apocalypses. Students of the New Testament are familiar through the Epistle to the Galatians [2] and the Revelation of St. John the Divine [3] with the idea of a heavenly Jerusalem of which the earthly was a material counterpart; and such conceptions found a 'locus classicus' within the pages of the Old Testament itself, in Exodus 25[40] (where Moses is enjoined to construct the Tabernacle and its appurtenances according to the pattern which was revealed to him on Mount Sinai), a verse which is quoted in Heb. 8[5] and is one of the main clues to the argument of the Epistle. The author, concerned to show that all the truth of Judaism is gathered up in the fuller revelation in Jesus Christ, eagerly seizes upon Exodus 25[40] as an indication that Judaism provided only 'carnal' [4] copies of 'things in the heavens' (Heb. 9[23]). Whereas (he says in 10[1]) the law had 'a shadow' of ultimate reality, in Christ we have its 'very image'.[5] To borrow the illuminating phrase of a recent theological work,[6] the Law was 'significant' of Reality, while Christ is 'expressive' of it. As is stated, for instance, in Heb. 10[3], the sacrifices of the Law represented the need of the forgiveness of sins, whereas Christ actually effected it.

We are now in a position to see more clearly the reason for what will have been suggested by the preceding essay, namely that in stating the Atonement the author is somewhat tied and bound by the terms of the Jewish sacrificial system. He is influenced throughout by his conception of that system as a copy of the Truth. For the same reason he sets forth Christ's work as the *real* Priesthood, as ministry in the *real* Tabernacle, as the inauguration of the *real* Covenant.

But it is when we arrive at chapter 11 that we understand that

[1] For the Alexandrian affinities of Hebrews see above, pp. 14, 17 ff.
[2] Gal. 4[26].                 [3] Rev. 21[2 ff.];
[4] See the use of 'carnal' in 7[16].
[5] See note on 10[1] and cf. 1[3].
[6] Canon Quick, *The Christian Sacraments* (Nisbet, 1927), pp. 26 ff.

this 'idealistic' mode of thought is for our author no mere deduction from Exodus 25⁴⁰, adopted for the sake of 'occasional' argument against Gnosticism or Judaism; for in that chapter faith, the very essence of the religious life, is said to consist in adherence to abiding spiritual realities (or, as we should say in modern phraseology, values), behind and beyond all the changes and chances of human history; while spiritual progress is a pilgrimage towards an 'unseen', 'hoped-for' 'city, whose builder and maker is God'.

## (d) *Eschatology*.

The eschatology of the epistle differs considerably from the conventional Jewish eschatology which New Testament writers generally adopted. The difference is due to the Platonism, the idealist philosophy, of the author, with its contrast between the heavenly world and the physical universe which is its shadow or copy. Whereas Jewish and Christian Apocalyptists envisaged the difference between imperfection and perfection primarily under categories of *time*, distinguishing between this age and the age to come, the language of Hebrews suggests categories of *space*, distinguishing between this world and the heavenly world of spiritual realities.[1] For the author of Hebrews the present reality of the heavenly sphere, the sphere into which Christ has passed and to which we are anchored,[2] is the fundamentally important fact. The Jewish Apocalyptists, on the other hand, and most early Christian thinkers in their train, concentrated on the future establishment of a heavenly kingdom in substitution for this present world order. It is a fundamental difference of emphasis, but we must be careful not to exaggerate it.

Like the Apocalypses, Hebrews looks forward to a time when this imperfect world order shall be abolished, 12²⁶ ᶠ· (see notes in commentary *ad loc.*), and when the true, spiritual order alone shall remain. Thus its author can the more readily, in 6⁵, describe his 'real' world in the current conventional terms as 'the age which is to come'. Further, no Christian in this

[1] See Dr. E. F. Scott, *The Epistle to the Hebrews*, chap. vi, Two Ages and Two Worlds.
[2] 6¹⁸⁻²⁰.

imperfect world can fail to adopt a forward-looking outlook. We may emphasize rightly the present reality of heavenly things, but we must emphasize also the fact that as yet we have imperfectly realized them. Thus we have in $9^{11}$ and $10^1$ (see notes *ad loc.*) the phrase 'good things *to come*'.

From the other side, the Apocalyptists themselves had affinities with Platonism. They imagined a true Jerusalem in the heavens to which St. Paul, for example, refers in Gal. $4^{26}$, and which corresponds with the heavenly city, the 'city which is to come' in Hebrews (e.g. $13^{14}$).

It remains, however, true that detailed eschatological speculation of the Apocalyptic type is ruled out of Hebrews by the dominating Platonism of its author's outlook. Like other New Testament writers he sees so clearly the divergence between the Truth as it is in Jesus and the world of his day that he feels that such acute tension cannot last long. He writes of 'the day approaching' ($10^{25}$, see note), and of an imminent judgement ($10^{27-31}$), but in vague and general terms. He is too aware of the greatness of our present possessions to have any taste for concentration on the 'Last Things'. When he writes of judgement in $9^{27}$ it is in terms which suggest an individual judgement passed on each man's life at its close rather than a general Judgement 'at the last day'. 'At the end of these days' ($1^2$) and 'now at the end of the ages' ($9^{26}$) are eschatological phrases, but they are dictated more by the author's desire to suggest the absolute finality of the revelation in Christ than by any sense of the imminence of the end of the world. (See notes in Commentary *ad loc.*). Finally, the Epistle contains two references to the second Advent of Christ.[1] The first is quite explicit and unmistakable, in $9^{28}$. But (see note *ad loc.*) the reference is due to the thought of the reappearing of the High Priest on the Day of Atonement rather than to the influence of Apocalyptic, and does not exactly accord with the picture, in $9^{12}$, of Christ as having entered once for all into the heavenly sanctuary. The whole theme of the Epistle is our pilgrimage to the heavenly city where Christ reigns 'on the right hand of God'. Naturally, therefore,

---

[1] $1^6$ is probably not such a reference. See note *ad loc.*

the writer does not dwell on the thought of His re-emergence from the sphere where his work is consummated and which is our spiritual fatherland. The reference to a Coming in $10^{37}$ is in the vaguest possible terms, borrowed from Habakkuk, and does not amount to more than the imminence of what we might call, with similar vagueness, a 'divine visitation'.

The language of Jesus Christ was much coloured by the eschatological phraseology of the Apocalyptists. But by His Life, Death, and teaching He so enriched human life as to give to the Kingdom of God a wealth of meaning relatively to the present age. Towards the bringing out of this present content of 'the kingdom' the author of Hebrews is, with St. John the Evangelist, one of the main contributors.

## (e) *Rigorism of the Epistle.*

The author of Hebrews expresses himself so strongly on the subject of sin as to appear to exclude all possibility of repentance and forgiveness for any deliberate wrongdoing. The relevant passages in the Epistle are $6^{4-8}$, $10^{26-31}$, $12^{15-17}$. The author's language on this subject is more uncompromising than that of any other New Testament writer and his attitude appears, at first sight, to be strangely different from that of Christ Himself. He is in danger, however, of being misunderstood and of receiving less than justice in this matter from the modern reader. His mind is focused to a large extent on the Jewish sacrificial system, and a glance at the theories underlying that system will help us to understand the apparently extreme rigorism of his epistle. In *The Theology of the Old Testament* (p. 315) Davidson writes:

'A distinction is drawn in the Old Testament . . . between sins of ignorance or inadvertence and sins done with a high hand or of purpose. . . . The former class embraced more than mere involuntary or inadvertent sins. The class comprehended all sins done not in a spirit of rebellion against the law or ordinance of Jehovah—sins committed through human imperfection, or human ignorance or human passion; sins done when the mind was diverted to some end connected with human weakness or elfishness, but not formally opposed to the Lawgiver. The distinction was thus primarily a distinction in regard to the state of mind of the transgressor. . . .

Only sins of ignorance were capable of being atoned for by sacrifice. . . . The sins done with a high hand threw those committing
them outside the Covenant relationship. They were an infraction of
the fundamental conditions of the covenant union. Such a sin as
idolatry, homage to another deity than Jehovah, infringed the first
principle of the covenant relation, the basis of which was that
Jehovah was the God of Israel.'

Of this distinction between 'sins of ignorance' and 'sins with
a high hand' and of the fact that the former alone were regarded
as capable of being atoned for by sacrifice [1] the author of Hebrews
shows himself aware. Not only have we, in $5^2$, 'able to bear
gently with the *ignorant and erring*' as one of the necessary
qualifications of a high priest, but in $9^7$ 'ignorances' (see marg.,
Greek ἀγνοημάτων) is the term with which he describes the offences
for which the Old Testament sacrifices were offered. Further,
in $10^{26}$ we read 'If we sin *willingly*' (the Greek word, ἐκουσίως,
has all the emphasis, standing first in the sentence) 'there remaineth no more a sacrifice for sins'. Noticing, then, the extent
to which the author of Hebrews has identified himself with the
Jewish theory and remembering the very wide connotation which
that theory gives to 'ignorances' and its restriction of deliberate
sin, practically, to sins involving an element of apostasy, we find
the apparent rigorism of Hebrews greatly mitigated. If we have
succeeded in Section B of this Introduction [2] in establishing
Jewish Gnosticism as the foe envisaged in Hebrews we shall
understand the fear of apostasy which haunts its author; and his
language about deliberate sin will become still more intelligible
when we remember that Gnosticism involved some of its ad-
herents in a departure not only from the Christian Faith but
from Christian morals as well.[3]

The above suppositions are borne out by a further examination
in detail of the rigoristic passages of the Epistle.

The 'falling away' contemplated in $6^6$, when examined in its
context, is seen to be an apostasy involving denial of the elements
of the faith outlined in $6^{1 f.}$. 'It would be a waste of time', says
the author in $6^{2-6}$,[4] 'to go over the elementary ground again, for,

[1] Num. $15^{27-30}$.    [2] Pp. 20 ff.    [3] See p. 23.
[4] See note on $6^4$.

if you have gone back on it, your case is hopeless.' Similarly, in
$10^{26-31}$, the instance from the Mosaic law with which (in $v^{28}$) the
author illustrates his point, is an instance of apostasy from true
doctrine, from the worship of 'Jehovah' to other gods. (See note
on $10^{28}$ in Commentary.) Notice also the strong language with
which, in $10^{29}$, the kind of sinner which the author has in mind is
described. He is one who has 'counted the blood of the covenant
a common thing'. Compare Davidson's statement that 'sins
done with a high hand threw those committing them outside the
covenant relationship. . . . Such a sin as idolatry, homage to
another deity than Jehovah, infringed the first principle of the
covenant relation.'[1]

Again, $12^{15}$ describes the sin of which the author is thinking as
a 'root of bitterness', a phrase borrowed from Deut. $29^{18}$, where
its significance is 'a heart that turneth away from the Lord our
God to go and serve the gods of other nations'.

The particular sin (fornication) specified in $12^{16}$, in connexion
with the danger of apostasy, is laid to the charge of the non-
ascetic type of Gnostic in Rev. $2^{14, \ 20-22}$, as well as by many
early Christian writers outside the New Testament.

## (f) *Characteristic words and phrases of Hebrews.*

The writer uses the *a fortiori* form of argument in $2^{2f}$, $9^{13f}$,
$10^{28f}$, $12^{25}$.

In the following places he deduces from *Old Testament* passages
the inadequacy of the Old Covenant and its ultimate abrogation:
$7^{11-13, \ 18}$, $8^{7-13}$, $10^{4-9}$.

*Promise.* Both the noun, in $4^1$, $6^{12, \ 15, \ 17}$, $7^6$, $8^6$, $9^{15}$, $10^{36}$, $11^9$ (twice),
$11^{13, \ 17, \ 33, \ 39}$, and the verb, in $6^{13}$, $10^{23}$, $11^{11}$, $12^{26}$. The frequency
of these words is to be connected with the writer's interest in
Old Testament prophecy, and with his conception of faith, which
is akin to hope.

'*To draw near*' (προσέρχεσθαι). See $4^{16}$, $7^{25}$, $10^1$, $10^{22}$, $11^6$, $12^{18}$,
$12^{22}$, cf. 'draw nigh' (ἐγγίζομεν) in $7^{19}$. These words are used in

---

[1] The parallelism is so striking that it is difficult to remember that
Davidson is not writing about the Epistle to the Hebrews but about Old
Testament Theology.

the sense of 'approaching' God, and illustrate the writer's fundamental conception of religion as worship.

'*Serve*' (λατρεύειν). See $8^5$, $9^9$, $9^{14}$, $10^2$, $12^{28}$, $13^{10}$. This is the technical, liturgical term for service in a sanctuary and illustrates therefore the same point as the use of 'draw near'.

'*Perfect*'. The adjective 'perfect' in $5^{14}$ and $9^{11}$. The abstract noun 'perfection' in $6^1$ and $7^{11}$. The noun 'perfecter' in $12^2$. The verb 'to perfect' in $2^{10}$, $5^9$, $7^{19}$, $7^{28}$, $9^9$, $10^1$, $10^{14}$, $11^{40}$, $12^{23}$. The words are used not of moral perfection but of the completion of a process. Their frequency is due to the writer's insistence on the absolute and final nature of the Christian Revelation. Christ, he says, was a *fully qualified* ('perfected') priest ($2^{10}$, $5^9$), through Him men can attain to a perfect worshipping relationship toward God (see e.g. $10^1$, $10^{14}$).

*To inherit*, $1^4$, $1^{14}$, $6^{12}$, $12^{17}$. *Inheritance*, $9^{15}$, $11^8$, *Heir*, $1^2$, $6^{17}$, $11^7$. Though emphasizing the absolute nature of the Christian revelation and the perfection of the relationship with God which is offered to us in Christ, the author of Hebrews insists that there are still 'good things to come'.[1] The Christian and even Christ Himself (see $1^2$ and note) have, secured to them, a wealth of possessions upon which they have not yet fully entered. 'Inheritance' emphasizes the initiative of the Father in the work of our salvation; and illustrates the forward-looking attitude of the Epistle, which represents life as a pilgrimage[2] or a race.[3]

'*Better*', '*more excellent*', '*greater*', in $1^4$, $3^3$, $6^9$, $7^7$, $7^{19}$, $7^{22}$, $8^6$, $9^{23}$, $10^{34}$, $11^4$, $11^{16}$, $11^{35}$, $11^{40}$, $12^{24}$; cf. 'more perfect' in $9^{11}$. The Epistle constantly states the superiority of Christianity to Judaism, or the superiority of the spiritual substance to its earthly shadow.

*The living God*, $3^{12}$, $9^{14}$, $10^{31}$, $12^{22}$; cf. the 'living Word' in $4^{12}$ and the 'living way' in $10^{20}$. Though the author's thought has affinities with Plato's idealism,[4] he escapes the least satisfactory element in Platonic thought, namely the impassivity of God. Christianity inherited from Judaism and enriched the belief in the activity of God Himself in human affairs.

---

[1] See $9^{11}$ and note.    [2] Chap. 11.    [3] $12^{1f}$.
[4] See pp. 40 ff.

# Leading Ideas of the Epistle 49

*Author* (ἀρχηγός), $2^{10}$, $12^2$. With this word, which is better translated 'pioneer',[1] the writer sums up his conception of Christ as the great Leader of humanity. The word is found elsewhere in the N.T. only in the earliest Christian sermons recorded in the Acts of the Apostles.[2]

*It is impossible*, $6^4$ (in the Greek, $6^6$ in the English text), $6^{18}$, $10^4$, $11^6$. The author's habit of thus stating what he regards as a self-evident absurdity is further illustrated by $9^{26}$.[3]

*Recompense of reward* (μισθαποδοσία) in $2^2$, $10^{35}$, and $11^{26}$; cf. 'Rewarder' (μισθαποδότης) in $11^6$. These words are not found elsewhere in the New Testament.

*Godly fear* (εὐλάβεια) $5^7$ and $12^{28}$; cf. the verb (εὐλαβηθείς) in $11^7$.

*Partaking of* (the adjective μέτοχος, or the verb, μετέχειν), $1^9$ (in quotation from Ps. $45^7$), $2^{14}$, $3^1$, $3^{14}$, $5^{13}$, $6^4$, $7^{13}$, $12^8$, μεταλαμβάνειν in $6^7$ and $12^{10}$. Some of these instances (e.g. $7^{13}$) represent a rather vague use of the phrase. A similar vagueness attaches to the phrase 'nigh unto cursing' in $6^8$ (cf. 'nigh unto vanishing' in $8^{13}$) and to 'things that accompany salvation' (ἐχόμενα σωτηρίας) in $6^9$, as well as to the words 'without sin' in $9^{28}$ (see note). Such vagueness is characteristic of one who is an orator rather than an exact thinker and writer.

*Boldness* (παρρησία), a frequent word in the New Testament, appears in $3^6$, $4^{16}$, $10^{19, 35}$. It accords well in this epistle with the author's exhortation to realize the all-sufficiency and finality of the revelation in Jesus Christ. See, further, note on $10^{19}$.

*Continually* (εἰς τὸ διηνεκές), $7^3$, $10^{1, 12, 14}$. Unique in the N.T.

## Note on the Text of the Epistle.

It has not been judged desirable or possible within the limits of this commentary to open up the subject of the textual criticism of Hebrews. Discussion of the various extant texts in order to be intelligible has to be lengthy. The most important variant readings are noticed in the notes on $4^2$, $9^1$, $9^{11}$, and $12^3$: it will be seen that in none of these cases is the textual question of much importance for the interpretation of the Epistle.

[1] See notes on $2^{10}$ and $12^2$.
[2] Acts $3^{15}$ and $5^{31}$.
[3] See note *ad loc.*

D

# BIBLIOGRAPHY

MOFFATT: *Hebrews.* International Critical Commentary Series.

WESTCOTT: *The Epistle to the Hebrews.*

DAVIDSON: *The Epistle to the Hebrews* (Handbooks for Bible Classes and Private Students).

PEAKE: *Hebrews* (The Century Bible).

NAIRNE: *Hebrews* (The Cambridge Bible).

WICKHAM: *The Epistle to the Hebrews* (Westminster Commentaries).

NAIRNE: *The Epistle of Priesthood.*

SCOTT: *The Epistle to the Hebrews.*

DU BOSE: *High Priesthood and Sacrifice.*

# THE EPISTLE OF PAUL THE APOSTLE TO THE

# HEBREWS

I$^{1-3}$. *Summary of the Christology of the Epistle.*

1 GOD, having of old time spoken unto the fathers in the
2 prophets by divers portions and in divers manners, hath at
the end of these days spoken unto us in $^1$*his* Son, whom he
appointed heir of all things, through whom also he made the
3 $^2$worlds; who being the effulgence of his glory, and $^3$the very
image of his substance, and upholding all things by the word
of his power, when he had made purification of sins, sat down
on the right hand of the Majesty on high;

I$^{4-14}$. *The Eternal Son greater than angels.*

4 Having become by so much better than the angels, as he
5 hath inherited a more excellent name than they. For unto
which of the angels said he at any time,

Thou art my Son,

This day have I begotten thee?

and again,

I will be to him a Father,

And he shall be to me a Son?

6 $^4$And when he again $^5$bringeth in the firstborn into $^6$the world
7 he saith, And let all the angels of God worship him. And of
the angels he saith,

Who maketh his angels $^7$winds,

And his ministers a flame of fire:

8 but of the Son *he saith,*

Thy throne, O God, is for ever and ever;

And the sceptre of uprightness is the sceptre of $^8$thy
kingdom.

9 Thou hast loved righteousness, and hated iniquity;

---

$^1$ Gr. *a Son.*  $^2$ Gr. *ages.*  $^3$ Or, *the impress of his substance*
$^4$ Or, *And again, when he bringeth in*  $^5$ Or, *shall have brought in*
$^6$ Gr. *the inhabited earth.*  $^7$ Or, *spirits*  $^8$ The two oldest Greek
manuscripts read *his.*

Therefore God, thy God, hath anointed thee
With the oil of gladness above thy fellows.

10 And,

Thou, Lord, in the beginning hast laid the foundation of
the earth,
And the heavens are the works of thy hands:

11 They shall perish; but thou continuest:
And they all shall wax old as doth a garment;

12 And as a mantle shalt thou roll them up,
As a garment, and they shall be changed:
But thou art the same,
And thy years shall not fail.

13 But of which of the angels hath he said at any time,
Sit thou on my right hand,
Till I make thine enemies the footstool of thy feet?

14 Are they not all ministering spirits, sent forth to do service for
the sake of them that shall inherit salvation?

2[1-4]. *Interlude of warning and exhortation based on the
preceding Section.*

2 Therefore we ought to give the more earnest heed to the
things that were heard, lest haply we drift away *from them.*

2 For if the word spoken through angels proved stedfast, and
every transgression and disobedience received a just recom-

3 pense of reward; how shall we escape, if we neglect so great
salvation? which having at the first been spoken through the

4 Lord, was confirmed unto us by them that heard; God also
bearing witness with them, both by signs and wonders, and
by manifold powers, and by [1]gifts of the [2]Holy Ghost, according to his own will.

2[5-18]. *The Human Christ greater than angels.*

5 For not unto angels did he subject [3]the world to come,
6 whereof we speak. But one hath somewhere testified, saying,

---

[1] Gr. *distributions.*    [2] Or, *Holy Spirit*: and so throughout this book.
[3] Gr. *the inhabited earth.*

What is man, that thou art mindful of him?
Or the son of man, that thou visitest him?

7 Thou madest him [1]a little lower than the angels;
Thou crownedst him with glory and honour,
[2]And didst set him over the works of thy hands:

8 Thou didst put all things in subjection under his feet.
For in that he subjected all things unto him, he left nothing
that is not subject to him. But now we see not yet all things
9 subjected to him. But we behold him who hath been made
[1]a little lower than the angels, *even* Jesus, because of the
suffering of death crowned with glory and honour, that by the
10 grace of God he should taste death for every *man*. For it
became him, for whom are all things, and through whom are
all things, [3]in bringing many sons unto glory, to make the
11 [4]author of their salvation perfect through sufferings. For both
he that sanctifieth and they that are sanctified are all of one:
for which cause he is not ashamed to call them brethren,
12 saying,

I will declare thy name unto my brethren,
In the midst of the [5]congregation will I sing thy praise.

13 And again, I will put my trust in him. And again, Behold,
14 I and the children which God hath given me. Since then the
children are sharers in [6]flesh and blood, he also himself in like
manner partook of the same; that through death he [7]might
bring to nought him that [8]had the power of death, that is,
15 the devil; and [7]might deliver all them who through fear of
16 death were all their lifetime subject to bondage. For verily
not of angels doth he take hold, but he taketh hold of the seed
17 of Abraham. Wherefore it behoved him in all things to be
made like unto his brethren, that he might be a merciful and
faithful high priest in things pertaining to God, to make
18 propitiation for the sins of the people. [9]For [10]in that he himself
hath suffered being tempted, he is able to succour them that
are tempted.

[1] Or, *for a little while lower*    [2] Many authorities omit *And didst ... hands.*
[3] Or, *having brought*    [4] Or, *captain*    [5] Or, *church*    [6] Gr. *blood and flesh.*
[7] Or, *may*    [8] Or, *hath*    [9] Or, *For having been himself tempted in that wherein he hath suffered*    [10] Or, *wherein*

### 3[1-6]. *Christ greater than Moses.*

**3** Wherefore, holy brethren, partakers of a heavenly calling, consider the Apostle and High Priest of our confession,
2 *even* Jesus; who was faithful to him that [1]appointed him, as
3 also was Moses in all [2]his house. For he hath been counted worthy of more glory than Moses, by so much as he that
4 [3]built the house hath more honour than the house. For every house is [3]builded by some one; but he that [3]built all things
5 is God. And Moses indeed was faithful in all [2]his house as a servant, for a testimony of those things which were after-
6 ward to be spoken; but Christ as a son, over [2]his house; whose house are we, if we hold fast our boldness and the glorying of our hope firm unto the end.

### 3[7]–4[13]. *Interlude of warning and exhortation based on the preceding Section.*

7　Wherefore, even as the Holy Ghost saith,
　　To-day if ye shall hear his voice,
8　　Harden not your hearts, as in the provocation,
　　Like as in the day of the temptation in the wilderness,
9　　[4]Wherewith your fathers tempted *me* by proving *me*,
　　And saw my works forty years.
10　　Wherefore I was displeased with this generation,
　　And said, They do alway err in their heart:
　　But they did not know my ways;
11　　As I sware in my wrath,
　　[5]They shall not enter into my rest.
12 Take heed, brethren, lest haply there shall be in any one of you an evil heart of unbelief, in falling away from the living God:
13 but exhort one another day by day, so long as it is called To-day; lest any one of you be hardened by the deceitfulness of
14 sin: for we are become partakers [6]of Christ, if we hold fast the
15 beginning of our confidence firm unto the end: while it is said,
　　To-day if ye shall hear his voice,
　　Harden not your hearts, as in the provocation.

[1] Gr. *made*.　[2] That is, *God's house*. See Num. xii. 7.　[3] Or, *established*
[4] Or, *Where*　[5] Gr. *If they shall enter*.　[6] Or, *with*

MICHELANGELO'S MOSES
S. Pietro in Vincoli, Rome

16 For who, when they heard, did provoke? nay, did not all they
17 that came out of Egypt by Moses? And with whom was he
displeased forty years? was it not with them that sinned,
18 whose ¹carcases fell in the wilderness? And to whom sware
he that they should not enter into his rest, but to them that
19 were disobedient? And we see that they were not able to enter
in because of unbelief.

4 Let us fear therefore, lest haply, a promise being left of
entering into his rest, any one of you should seem to have
2 come short of it. For indeed we have had ²good tidings
preached unto us, even as also they: but the word of hearing
did not profit them, because ³they were not united by faith
3 with them that heard. ⁴For we which have believed do enter
into that rest; even as he hath said,

As I sware in my wrath,
⁵They shall not enter into my rest:

although the works were finished from the foundation of the
4 world. For he hath said somewhere of the seventh *day* on this
wise, And God rested on the seventh day from all his works;
5 and in this *place* again,

⁵They shall not enter into my rest.

6 Seeing therefore it remaineth that some should enter thereinto,
and they to whom ⁶the good tidings were before preached failed
7 to enter in because of disobedience, he again defineth a certain
day, ⁷saying in David, after so long a time, To-day, as it hath
been before said,

To-day if ye shall hear his voice,
Harden not your hearts.

8 For if ⁸Joshua had given them rest, he would not have spoken
9 afterward of another day. There remaineth therefore a sabbath
10 rest for the people of God. For he that is entered into his rest
hath himself also rested from his works, as God did from his.
11 Let us therefore give diligence to enter into that rest, that no

---

¹ Gr. *limbs.*    ² Or, *a gospel*    ³ Some ancient authorities read *it was.*
⁴ Some ancient authorities read *We therefore.*    ⁵ Gr. *If they shall enter.*
⁶ Or, *the gospel was*    ⁷ Or, *To-day, saying in David, after so long a time,
as it hath been &c.*    ⁸ Gr. *Jesus.*

12 man fall ¹after the same example of disobedience. For the word
of God is living, and active, and sharper than any two-edged
sword, and piercing even to the dividing of soul and spirit, of
both joints and marrow, and quick to discern the thoughts
13 and intents of the heart. And there is no creature that is not
manifest in his sight: but all things are naked and laid open
before the eyes of him with whom we have to do.

4¹⁴–5¹⁰. *Beginning of the setting forth of Christ as High Priest.*

14    Having then a great high priest, who hath passed through
the heavens, Jesus the Son of God, let us hold fast our confes-
15 sion. For we have not a high priest that cannot be touched
with the feeling of our infirmities; but one that hath been in all
16 points tempted like as *we are, yet* without sin. Let us therefore
draw near with boldness unto the throne of grace, that we may
receive mercy, and may find grace to help *us* in time of need.

5 For every high priest, being taken from among men, is appointed for men in things pertaining to God, that he may offer
2 both gifts and sacrifices for sins: who can bear gently with the
ignorant and erring, for that he himself also is compassed with
3 infirmity; and by reason thereof is bound, as for the people, so
4 also for himself, to offer for sins. And no man taketh the honour
unto himself, but when he is called of God, even as was Aaron.
5 So Christ also glorified not himself to be made a high priest, but
he that spake unto him,

Thou art my Son,
This day have I begotten thee:
6 as he saith also in another *place*,

Thou art a priest for ever
After the order of Melchizedek.

7 Who in the days of his flesh, having offered up prayers and
supplications with strong crying and tears unto him that was
able to save him ²from death, and having been heard for his
8 godly fear, though he was a Son, yet learned obedience by the
9 things which he suffered; and having been made perfect, he
became unto all them that obey him the ³author of eternal

---

¹ Or, *into* Gr. *in.*    ² Or, *out of*    ³ Gr. *cause.*

10 salvation; named of God a high priest after the order of Melchizedek.

**5[11]-6[20]. *Digression to arouse the readers out of their dullness.***

11 Of [1]whom we have many things to say, and hard of in-
12 terpretation, seeing ye are become dull of hearing. For when by reason of the time ye ought to be teachers, ye have need again [2]that some one teach you the rudiments of the [3]first principles of the oracles of God; and are become such as have need of
13 milk, and not of solid food. For every one that partaketh of milk is without experience of the word of righteousness; for he
14 is a babe. But solid food is for [4]fullgrown men, *even* those who by reason of use have their senses exercised to discern good and evil.

6 Wherefore let us [5]cease to speak of the first principles of Christ, and press on unto [6]perfection; not laying again a foundation of repentance from dead works, and of faith toward
2 God, [7]of the teaching of [8]baptisms, and of laying on of hands,
3 and of resurrection of the dead, and of eternal judgement. And
4 this will we do, if God permit. For as touching those who were once enlightened [9]and tasted of the heavenly gift, and were
5 made partakers of the Holy Ghost, and [10]tasted the good word
6 of God, and the powers of the age to come, and *then* fell away, it is impossible to renew them again unto repentance; [11]seeing they crucify to themselves the Son of God afresh, and put him to
7 an open shame. For the land which hath drunk the rain that cometh oft upon it, and bringeth forth herbs meet for them for whose sake it is also tilled, receiveth blessing from God:
8 but if it beareth thorns and thistles, it is rejected and nigh unto a curse; whose end is to be burned.

9 But, beloved, we are persuaded better things of you, and
10 things that [12]accompany salvation, though we thus speak: for

[1] Or, *which*  [2] Or, *that* one *teach you which* be *the rudiments*  [3] Gr. *beginning*  [4] Or, *perfect*  [5] Gr. *leave the word of the beginning of Christ.*  [6] Or, *full growth*  [7] Some ancient authorities read, even *the teaching of.*  [8] Or, *washings*  [9] Or, *having both tasted of . . . and being made . . . and having tasted &c.*  [10] Or, *tasted the word of God that it is good*  [11] Or, *the while*  [12] Or, *are near to*

God is not unrighteous to forget your work and the love which
ye shewed toward his name, in that ye ministered unto the
11 saints, and still do minister. And we desire that each one of
you may shew the same diligence unto the ¹fulness of hope
12 even to the end: that ye be not sluggish, but imitators of them
who through faith and patience inherit the promises.
13    For when God made promise to Abraham, since he could
14 swear by none greater, he sware by himself, saying, Surely
blessing I will bless thee, and multiplying I will multiply thee.
15 And thus, having patiently endured, he obtained the promise.
16 For men swear by the greater: and in every dispute of theirs

Part of a Roman anchor of the first century A.D. The anchor is of lead,
and the name of the ship is engraved upon it ('Zeus Hypatos' abbreviated)

17 the oath is final for confirmation. Wherein God, being minded
to shew more abundantly unto the heirs of the promise the im-
18 mutability of his counsel, ²interposed with an oath: that by
two immutable things, in which it is impossible for God to lie,
we may have a strong encouragement, who have fled for refuge
19 to lay hold of the hope set before us; which we have as an
anchor of the soul, *a hope* both sure and stedfast and entering
20 into that which is within the veil; whither as a forerunner
Jesus entered for us, having become a high priest for ever after
the order of Melchizedek.

### 7¹⁻³. *The meaning of Christ's Priesthood after the Order of Melchizedek.*

7 For this Melchizedek, king of Salem, priest of God Most
High, who met Abraham returning from the slaughter of
2 the kings, and blessed him, to whom also Abraham divided

¹ Or, *full assurance*        ² Gr. *mediated.*

a tenth part of all (being first, by interpretation, King of righteousness, and then also King of Salem, which is, King of

3 peace; without father, without mother, without genealogy, having neither beginning of days nor end of life, but made like unto the Son of God), abideth a priest continually.

## 7[4-10]. *The Melchizedek priesthood greater than the Levitical.*

4      Now consider how great this man was, unto whom Abraham,
5 the patriarch, gave a tenth out of the chief spoils. And they indeed of the sons of Levi that receive the priest's office have commandment to take tithes of the people according to the law, that is, of their brethren, though these have come out of
6 the loins of Abraham: but he whose genealogy is not counted from them hath taken tithes of Abraham, and hath blessed
7 him that hath the promises. But without any dispute the less
8 is blessed of the better. And here men that die receive tithes;
9 but there one, of whom it is witnessed that he liveth. And, so to say, through Abraham even Levi, who receiveth tithes, hath
10 paid tithes; for he was yet in the loins of his father, when Melchizedek met him.

## 7[11-25]. *The Melchizedek priesthood supersedes the Levitical and the Law inextricably bound up with the Levitical priesthood.*

11      Now if there was perfection through the Levitical priesthood (for under it hath the people received the law), what further need *was there* that another priest should arise after the order of Melchizedek, and not be reckoned after the order of Aaron?
12 For the priesthood being changed, there is made of necessity
13 a change also [1]of the law. For he of whom these things are said [2]belongeth to another tribe, from which no man hath given
14 attendance at the altar. For it is evident that our Lord hath sprung out of Judah; as to which tribe Moses spake nothing
15 concerning priests. And *what we say* is yet more abundantly evident, if after the likeness of Melchizedek there ariseth
16 another priest, who hath been made, not after the law of

[1] Or, *of law*      [2] Gr. *hath partaken of.* See ch. ii. 14.

a carnal commandment, but after the power of an [1]endless
17 life: for it is witnessed *of him,*

> Thou art a priest for ever
> After the order of Melchizedek.

18 For there is a disannulling of a foregoing commandment
19 because of its weakness and unprofitableness (for the law made
nothing perfect), and a bringing in thereupon of a better hope,
20 through which we draw nigh unto God. And inasmuch as *it is*
21 not without the taking of an oath (for they indeed have been
made priests without an oath; but he with an oath [2]by him that
saith [3]of him,

> The Lord sware and will not repent himself,
> Thou art a priest for ever);

22 by so much also hath Jesus become the surety of a better
23 [4]covenant. And they indeed have been made priests many
in number, because that by death they are hindered from
24 continuing: but he, because he abideth for ever, [5]hath his
25 priesthood [6]unchangeable. Wherefore also he is able to save
[7]to the uttermost them that draw near unto God through him,
seeing he ever liveth to make intercession for them.

### 7[26-28]. *Our need of such an eternal High Priest.*

26    For such a high priest became us, holy, guileless, undefiled,
separated from sinners, and made higher than the heavens;
27 who needeth not daily, like those high priests, to offer up
sacrifices, first for his own sins, and then for the *sins* of the
people: for this he did once for all, when he offered up himself.
28 For the law appointeth men high priests, having infirmity; but
the word of the oath, which was after the law, *appointeth* a Son,
perfected for evermore.

### 8[1-5]. *The Tabernacle in which our High Priest ministers.*

8 [8]Now [9]in the things which we are saying the chief point *is
this*: We have such a high priest, who sat down on the right

---

[1] Gr. *indissoluble.*   [2] Or, *through*   [3] Or, *unto*   [4] Or, *testament*   [5] Or, *hath
a priesthood that doth not pass to another*   [6] Or, *inviolable*   [7] Gr. *completely.*
[8] Or, *Now to sum up what we are saying: We have &c.*   [9] Gr. *upon.*

2 hand of the throne of the Majesty in the heavens, a minister
of ¹the sanctuary, and of the true tabernacle, which the Lord
3 pitched, not man. For every high priest is appointed to offer
both gifts and sacrifices: wherefore it is necessary that this
4 *high priest* also have somewhat to offer. Now if he were on
earth, he would not be a priest at all, seeing there are those who
5 offer the gifts according to the law; who serve *that which is*
a copy and shadow of the heavenly things, even as Moses is
warned *of God* when he is about to ²make the tabernacle:
for, See, saith he, that thou make all things according to the
pattern that was shewed thee in the mount.

8⁶⁻¹³. *The New Covenant which our High Priest mediates.*

6    But now hath he obtained a ministry the more excellent,
by how much also he is the mediator of a better ³covenant,
7 which hath been enacted upon better promises. For if that
first *covenant* had been faultless, then would no place have been
8 sought for a second. For finding fault with them, he saith,
        Behold, the days come, saith the Lord,
        That I will ⁴make a new ³covenant with the house of Israel
            and with the house of Judah;
9        Not according to the ³covenant that I made with their
            fathers
        In the day that I took them by the hand to lead them
            forth out of the land of Egypt;
        For they continued not in my ³covenant,
        And I regarded them not, saith the Lord.
10       For this is the ³covenant that ⁵I will make with the house
            of Israel
        After those days, saith the Lord;
        I will put my laws into their mind,
        And on their heart also will I write them:
        And I will be to them a God,
        And they shall be to me a people:
11       And they shall not teach every man his fellow-citizen,

¹ Or, *holy things*    ² Or, *complete*    ³ Or, *testament*    ⁴ Gr. *accomplish.*
⁵ Gr. *I will covenant.*

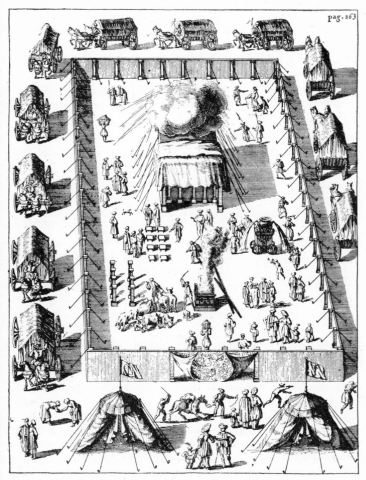

pag. 263

The Tabernacle, appurtenances, curtains, and wagons (Exodus xxv–xxvii). The transport was in the hands of the Levites (Numbers iii, vii. 3–9). The curious figures in the foreground will be noted: two men are bowing to each other, on the left; on the right one man is firing a pistol at a fugitive. From Leusden's *Philologus Hebreo-mixtus* (Utrecht, 1682)

And every man his brother, saying, Know the Lord:
For all shall know me,
From the least to the greatest of them.

12 For I will be merciful to their iniquities,
And their sins will I remember no more.

13 In that he saith, A new *covenant*, he hath made the first old. But that which is becoming old and waxeth aged is nigh unto vanishing away.

### 9$^{1-10}$. *Futility of the sacrifices under the Old Covenant.*

9 Now even the first *covenant* had ordinances of divine service, 2 and its sanctuary, *a sanctuary* of this world. For there was a tabernacle prepared, the first, wherein ¹*were* the candlestick, and the table, and ²the shewbread; which is called the Holy 3 place. And after the second veil, the tabernacle which is called 4 the Holy of holies; having a golden ³censer, and the ark of the covenant overlaid round about with gold, wherein ⁴*was* a golden pot holding the manna, and Aaron's rod that budded, and the 5 tables of the covenant; and above it cherubim of glory overshadowing ⁵the mercy-seat; of which things we cannot now 6 speak severally. Now these things having been thus prepared, the priests go in continually into the first tabernacle, accom- 7 plishing the services; but into the second the high priest alone, once in the year, not without blood, which he offereth for 8 himself, and for the ⁶errors of the people: the Holy Ghost this signifying, that the way into the holy place hath not yet been made manifest, while as the first tabernacle is yet standing; 9 which *is* a parable for the time *now* present; according to which are offered both gifts and sacrifices that cannot, as touching 10 the conscience, make the worshipper perfect, *being* only (with meats and drinks and divers washings) carnal ordinances, imposed until a time of reformation.

¹ Or, are   ² Gr. *the setting forth of the loaves.*   ³ Or, *altar of incense*
⁴ Or, is   ⁵ Gr. *the propitiatory.*   ⁶ Gr. *ignorances.*

The seven-branched candlestick, carried in triumph through Rome after the sack of Jerusalem. Relief on the arch of Titus

$9^{11}$–$10^{18}$. *The efficacy of the sacrifice of our High Priest contrasted with the old sacrifices.*

11    But Christ having come a high priest of [1]the good things to come, through the greater and more perfect tabernacle, not
12 made with hands, that is to say, not of this creation, nor yet through the blood of goats and calves, but through his own blood, entered in once for all into the holy place, having
13 obtained eternal redemption. For if the blood of goats and bulls, and the ashes of a heifer sprinkling them that have been
14 defiled, sanctify unto the cleanness of the flesh: how much more shall the blood of Christ, who through the eternal Spirit offered himself without blemish unto God, cleanse [2]your
15 conscience from dead works to serve the living God? And for this cause he is the mediator of a new [3]covenant, that a death having taken place for the redemption of the transgressions that were under the first [3]covenant, they that have been called
16 may receive the promise of the eternal inheritance. For where a [3]testament is, there must of necessity [4]be the death of him
17 that made it. For a [3]testament is of force [5]where there hath been death: [6]for doth it ever avail while he that made it liveth?
18 Wherefore even the first *covenant* hath not been dedicated
19 without blood. For when every commandment had been spoken by Moses unto all the people according to the law, he took the blood of the calves and the goats, with water and scarlet wool and hyssop, and sprinkled both the book itself,
20 and all the people, saying, This is the blood of the [3]covenant
21 which God commanded to you-ward. Moreover the tabernacle and all the vessels of the ministry he sprinkled in like manner
22 with the blood. And according to the law, I may almost say, all things are cleansed with blood, and apart from shedding of blood there is no remission.
23    It was necessary therefore that the copies of the things in the heavens should be cleansed with these; but the heavenly

---

[1] Some ancient authorities read *the good things that are come.*    [2] Many ancient authorities read *our.*    [3] The Greek word here used signifies both *covenant* and *testament.*    [4] Gr. *be brought.*    [5] Gr. *over the dead.*    [6] Or, *for it doth never . . . liveth.*

24 things themselves with better sacrifices than these. For Christ entered not into a holy place made with hands, like in pattern to the true; but into heaven itself, now to appear before the 25 face of God for us: nor yet that he should offer himself often; as the high priest entereth into the holy place year by year 26 with blood not his own; else must he often have suffered since the foundation of the world: but now once at the [1]end of the ages hath he been manifested to put away sin [2]by the sacrifice 27 of himself. And inasmuch as it is [3]appointed unto men once to 28 die, and after this *cometh* judgement; so Christ also, having been once offered to bear the sins of many, shall appear a second time, apart from sin, to them that wait for him, unto salvation.

10 For the law having a shadow of the good *things* to come, not the very image of the things, [4]they can never with the same sacrifices year by year, which they offer continually, make 2 perfect them that draw nigh. Else would they not have ceased to be offered, because the worshippers, having been once 3 cleansed, would have had no more conscience of sins? But in those *sacrifices* there is a remembrance made of sins year by 4 year. For it is impossible that the blood of bulls and goats 5 should take away sins. Wherefore when he cometh into the world, he saith,

> Sacrifice and offering thou wouldest not,
> But a body didst thou prepare for me;
6      In whole burnt offerings and *sacrifices* for sin thou hadst no pleasure:
7      Then said I, Lo, I am come
> (In the roll of the book it is written of me)
> To do thy will, O God.

8 Saying above, Sacrifices and offerings and whole burnt offerings and *sacrifices* for sin thou wouldest not, neither hadst pleasure therein (the which are offered according to the law), then hath 9 he said, Lo, I am come to do thy will. He taketh away the 10 first, that he may establish the second. [5]By which will we

---

[1] Or, *consummation*      [2] Or, *by his sacrifice.*      [3] Gr. *laid up for.*
[4] Some ancient authorities read *it can.*      [5] Or, *In*

have been sanctified through the offering of the body of Jesus
11 Christ once for all. And every [1]priest indeed standeth day by
day ministering and offering oftentimes the same sacrifices,
12 the which can never take away sins: but he, when he had
offered one sacrifice for [2]sins for ever, sat down on the right
13 hand of God; from henceforth expecting till his enemies be
14 made the footstool of his feet. For by one offering he hath
15 perfected for ever them that are sanctified. And the Holy
Ghost also beareth witness to us: for after he hath said,

16      This is the [3]covenant that [4]I will make with them
        After those days, saith the Lord;
        I will put my laws on their heart,
        And upon their mind also will I write them;
   *then saith he,*

17      And their sins and their iniquities will I remember no
        more.

18 Now where remission of these is, there is no more offering for
sin.

### $10^{19-25}$.  *Exhortation based on preceding sections.*

19      Having therefore, brethren, boldness to enter into the holy
20 place by the blood of Jesus, by the way which he dedicated for
us, a new and living way, through the veil, that is to say, his
21 flesh; and *having* a great priest over the house of God;
22 let us draw near with a true heart in [5]fulness of faith, having
our hearts sprinkled from an evil [6]conscience, and our body
23 washed with pure water: let us hold fast the confession of our
hope that it waver not; for he is faithful that promised:
24 and let us consider one another to provoke unto love and good
25 works; not forsaking the assembling of ourselves together, as
the custom of some is, but exhorting *one another*; and so much
the more, as ye see the day drawing nigh.

[1] Some ancient authorities read *high priest*.   [2] Or, *sins, for ever sat down
&c.*   [3] Or, *testament*   [4] Gr. *I will covenant.*   [5] Or, *full assurance*   [6] Or,
*conscience: and having our body washed with pure water, let us hold fast*

## $10^{26-31}$. *The fearfulness of apostasy.*

26 For if we sin wilfully after that we have received the knowledge of the truth, there remaineth no more a sacrifice for sins,
27 but a certain fearful expectation of judgement, and a [1]fierceness
28 of fire which shall devour the adversaries. A man that hath set at nought Moses' law dieth without compassion on *the word*
29 *of* two or three witnesses: of how much sorer punishment, think ye, shall he be judged worthy, who hath trodden under foot the Son of God, and hath counted the blood of the covenant, wherewith he was sanctified, [2]an unholy thing, and
30 hath done despite unto the Spirit of grace? For we know him that said, Vengeance belongeth unto me, I will recompense.
31 And again, The Lord shall judge his people. It is a fearful thing to fall into the hands of the living God.

## $10^{32-37}$. *Fall not at the eleventh hour from your former faith.*

32 But call to remembrance the former days, in which, after ye were enlightened, ye endured a great conflict of sufferings;
33 partly, being made a gazingstock both by reproaches and afflictions; and partly, becoming partakers with them that
34 were so used. For ye both had compassion on them that were in bonds, and took joyfully the spoiling of your possessions, knowing [3]that [4]ye yourselves have a better possession and an
35 abiding one. Cast not away therefore your boldness, which
36 hath great recompense of reward. For ye have need of patience, that, having done the will of God, ye may receive the promise.
37 For yet a very little while,
He that cometh shall come, and shall not tarry.

## $10^{38}-11^{40}$. *What faith is and what it can achieve.*

38 But [5]my righteous one shall live by faith:
And if he shrink back, my soul hath no pleasure in him.
39 But we are not [6]of them that shrink back unto perdition; but of them that have faith unto the [7]saving of the soul.

[1] Or, *jealousy*    [2] Gr. *a common thing.*    [3] Or, *that ye have your own selves for a better possession*    [4] Some ancient authorities read *ye have for yourselves a better possession.*    [5] Some ancient authorities read *the righteous one.* [6] Gr. *of shrinking back . . . but of faith.*    [7] Or, *gaining*

**11** Now faith is ¹the assurance of *things* hoped for, the ²prov-
2 ing of things not seen. For therein the elders had witness
3 borne to them. By faith we understand that the ³worlds have
been framed by the word of God, so that what is seen hath not
4 been made out of things which do appear. By faith Abel
offered unto God a more excellent sacrifice than Cain, through
which he had witness borne to him that he was righteous, ⁴God
bearing witness in ⁵respect of his gifts: and through it he
5 being dead yet speaketh. By faith Enoch was translated that
he should not see death; and he was not found, because God
translated him: for before his translation he hath had witness
6 borne to him that he had been well-pleasing unto God: and
without faith it is impossible to be well-pleasing *unto him*: for
he that cometh to God must believe that he is, and *that* he is
7 a rewarder of them that seek after him. By faith Noah, being
warned *of God* concerning things not seen as yet, moved with
godly fear, prepared an ark to the saving of his house; through
which he condemned the world, and became heir of the
8 righteousness which is according to faith. By faith Abraham,
when he was called, obeyed to go out unto a place which he
was to receive for an inheritance; and he went out, not knowing
9 whither he went. By faith he became a sojourner in the land
of promise, as in a *land* not his own, ⁶dwelling in tents, with
10 Isaac and Jacob, the heirs with him of the same promise: for
he looked for the city which hath the foundations, whose
11 ⁷builder and maker is God. By faith even Sarah herself received power to conceive seed when she was past age, since
12 she counted him faithful who had promised: wherefore also
there sprang of one, and him as good as dead, *so many* as the
stars of heaven in multitude, and as the sand, which is by the
sea shore, innumerable.
13 These all died in ⁸faith, not having received the promises,
but having seen them and greeted them from afar, and
having confessed that they were strangers and pilgrims on the

¹ Or, *the giving substance to* ² Or, *test* ³ Gr. *ages*. ⁴ The Greek
text in this clause is somewhat uncertain. ⁵ Or, *over his gifts* ⁶ Or,
*having taken up his abode in tents* ⁷ Or, *architect* ⁸ Gr. *according to.*

14 earth. For they that say such things make it manifest that
15 they are seeking after a country of their own. And if indeed
they had been mindful of that *country* from which they went
16 out, they would have had opportunity to return. But now

The story of Cain and Abel. From Ghiberti's 'Gates of Paradise' at Florence

they desire a better *country*, that is, a heavenly: wherefore God
is not ashamed of them, to be called their God: for he hath
prepared for them a city.

17    By faith Abraham, being tried, [1]offered up Isaac: yea, he
that had gladly received the promises was offering up his only

[1] Gr. *hath offered up*.

18 begotten *son*; *even he* ¹to whom it was said, In Isaac shall thy
19 seed be called: accounting that God *is* able to raise up, even
from the dead; from whence he did also in a parable receive
20 him back. By faith Isaac blessed Jacob and Esau, even con-
21 cerning things to come. By faith Jacob, when he was a dying,
blessed each of the sons of Joseph; and worshipped, *leaning*
22 upon the top of his staff. By faith Joseph, when his end was
nigh, made mention of the departure of the children of Israel;
23 and gave commandment concerning his bones. By faith Moses,
when he was born, was hid three months by his parents,
because they saw he was a goodly child; and they were not
24 afraid of the king's commandment. By faith Moses, when he
was grown up, refused to be called the son of Pharaoh's
25 daughter; choosing rather to be evil entreated with the people
26 of God, than to enjoy the pleasures of sin for a season; accounting the reproach of ²Christ greater riches than the treasures of
27 Egypt: for he looked unto the recompense of reward. By faith
he forsook Egypt, not fearing the wrath of the king; for he
28 endured, as seeing him who is invisible. By faith he ³kept the
passover, and the sprinkling of the blood, that the destroyer
29 of the firstborn should not touch them. By faith they passed
through the Red sea as by dry land: which the Egyptians
30 assaying to do were swallowed up. By faith the walls of
Jericho fell down, after they had been compassed about for
31 seven days. By faith Rahab the harlot perished not with them
that were disobedient, having received the spies with peace.
32 And what shall I more say? for the time will fail me if I tell of
Gideon, Barak, Samson, Jephthah; of David and Samuel and
33 the prophets: who through faith subdued kingdoms, wrought
righteousness, obtained promises, stopped the mouths of lions,
34 quenched the power of fire, escaped the edge of the sword,
from weakness were made strong, waxed mighty in war, turned
35 to flight armies of aliens. Women received their dead by a
resurrection: and others were ⁴tortured, not accepting ⁵their
36 deliverance; that they might obtain a better resurrection; and

---

¹ Or, *of*     ² Or, *the Christ*     ³ Or, *instituted* Gr. *hath made*.     ⁴ Or,
*beaten to death*     ⁵ Gr. *the redemption*.

A village in the desert. The Arab township of Siwa

A nomad encampment in Palestine

LIFE IN THE DESERT

others had trial of mockings and scourgings, yea, moreover of
37 bonds and imprisonment: they were stoned, they were sawn
asunder, they were tempted, they were slain with the sword:
they went about in sheepskins, in goatskins; being destitute,
38 afflicted, evil entreated (of whom the world was not worthy),
wandering in deserts and mountains and caves, and the holes
39 of the earth. And these all, having had witness borne to them
40 through their faith, received not the promise, God having
¹provided some better thing concerning us, that apart from us
they should not be made perfect.

12¹⁻¹³. *Helps in running the hard race.*

**12** Therefore let us also, seeing we are compassed about
with so great a cloud of witnesses, lay aside ²every weight,
and the sin which ³doth so easily beset us, and let us run with
2 patience the race that is set before us, looking unto Jesus the
⁴author and perfecter of *our* faith, who for the joy that was set
before him endured the cross, despising shame, and hath sat
3 down at the right hand of the throne of God. For consider him
that hath endured such gainsaying of sinners against ⁵them-
4 selves, that ye wax not weary, fainting in your souls. Ye have
5 not yet resisted unto blood, striving against sin: and ye have
forgotten the exhortation, which reasoneth with you as with sons,

My son, regard not lightly the chastening of the Lord,
Nor faint when thou art reproved of him;
6　　For whom the Lord loveth he chasteneth,
And scourgeth every son whom he receiveth.

7 ⁶It is for chastening that ye endure; God dealeth with you as
with sons; for what son is there whom *his* father chasteneth
8 not? But if ye are without chastening, whereof all have been
9 made partakers, then are ye bastards, and not sons. Furthermore, we had the fathers of our flesh to chasten us, and we
gave them reverence: shall we not much rather be in subjection
10 unto the Father of ⁷spirits, and live? For they verily for a few
days chastened *us* as seemed good to them; but he for *our*

¹ Or, *foreseen*　² Or, *all cumbrance*　³ Or, *doth closely cling to us* Or, *is
admired of many*　⁴ Or, *captain*　⁵ Many authorities, some ancient, read
*himself.*　⁶ Or, *Endure unto chastening*　⁷ Or, *our spirits*

'Wandering in deserts and mountains.' The great gate leading to the Wady Firán (on the probable route of the Exodus)

11 profit, that *we* may be partakers of his holiness. All chastening seemeth for the present to be not joyous, but grievous: yet afterward it yieldeth peaceable fruit unto them that have been
12 exercised thereby, *even the fruit* of righteousness. Wherefore
13 ¹lift up the hands that hang down, and the palsied knees; and make straight paths for your feet, that that which is lame be not ²turned out of the way, but rather be healed.

### 12¹⁴⁻¹⁷. *Your sanctification must not be compromised.*

14 Follow after peace with all men, and the sanctification with-
15 out which no man shall see the Lord: looking carefully ³lest *there be* any man that ⁴falleth short of the grace of God; lest any root of bitterness springing up trouble *you*, and thereby
16 the many be defiled; ³lest *there be* any fornicator, or profane person, as Esau, who for one mess of meat sold his own birth-
17 right. For ye know that even when he afterward desired to inherit the blessing, he was rejected (for he found no place of repentance), though he sought it diligently with tears.

### 12¹⁸⁻²⁹. *Sinai and Zion.*

18 For ye are not come unto ⁵*a mount* that might be touched, and that burned with fire, and unto blackness, and darkness,
19 and tempest, and the sound of a trumpet, and the voice of words; which *voice* they that heard intreated that no word
20 more should be spoken unto them: for they could not endure that which was enjoined, If even a beast touch the mountain,
21 it shall be stoned; and so fearful was the appearance, *that*
22 Moses said, I exceedingly fear and quake: but ye are come unto mount Zion, and unto the city of the living God, the heavenly
23 Jerusalem, ⁶and to ⁷innumerable hosts of angels, to the general assembly and church of the firstborn who are enrolled in heaven, and to God the Judge of all, and to the spirits of
24 just men made perfect, and to Jesus the mediator of a new ⁸covenant, and to the blood of sprinkling that speaketh better
25 ⁹than *that of* Abel. See that ye refuse not him that speaketh.

¹ Gr. *make straight.*   ² Or, *put out of joint*   ³ Or, *whether*   ⁴ Or, *falleth back from*   ⁵ Or, *a palpable and kindled fire*   ⁶ Or, *and to innumerable hosts, the general assembly of angels, and the church &c.*   ⁷ Gr. *myriads of angels.*   ⁸ Or. *testament*   ⁹ Or. *than Abel*

The summit of Jebel Musa, traditionally supposed
to be the place where Jehovah spoke with Moses

The plain of Er Ráhah, with Ras Safsáfeh, a spur of Jebel Musa, on the right

SINAI

For if they escaped not, when they refused him that warned *them* on earth, much more *shall not* we *escape*, who turn away
26 from him [1]that *warneth* from heaven: whose voice then shook the earth: but now he hath promised, saying, Yet once more will I make to tremble not the earth only, but also the heaven.
27 And this *word*, Yet once more, signifieth the removing of those things that are shaken, as of things that have been made, that
28 those things which are not shaken may remain. Wherefore, receiving a kingdom that cannot be shaken, let us have [2]grace,
29 whereby we may offer service well-pleasing to God with [3]reverence and awe: for our God is a consuming fire.

### 13[1-6]. *Ethical precepts.*

2 **13** Let love of the brethren continue. Forget not to shew love unto strangers: for thereby some have entertained angels
3 unawares. Remember them that are in bonds, as bound with them; them that are evil entreated, as being yourselves also in
4 the body. *Let* marriage *be* had in honour among all, and *let* the bed *be* undefiled: for fornicators and adulterers God will
5 judge. [4]Be ye free from the love of money; content with such things as ye have: for himself hath said, I will in no wise fail
6 thee, neither will I in any wise forsake thee. So that with good courage we say,

The Lord is my helper; I will not fear:
What shall man do unto me?

### 13[7-9]. *Remember your first Christian teachers and the faith they held.*

7 Remember them that had the rule over you, which spake unto you the word of God; and considering the issue of their
8 [5]life, imitate their faith. Jesus Christ *is* the same yesterday
9 and to-day, *yea* and [6]for ever. Be not carried away by divers and strange teachings: for it is good that the heart be stablished by grace; not by meats, wherein they that [7]occupied themselves were not profited.

[1] Or, *that is from heaven*   [2] Or, *thankfulness*   [3] Or, *godly fear*   [4] Gr. Let *your turn* of mind be *free*.   [5] Gr. *manner of life*.   [6] Gr. *unto the ages*.
[7] Gr. *walked*.

### $13^{10-14}$. *Judaism is superseded and must be left behind.*

10 We have an altar, whereof they have no right to eat which
11 serve the tabernacle. For the bodies of those beasts, whose
blood is brought into the holy place [1]by the high priest *as*
12 *an offering* for sin, are burned without the camp. Wherefore
Jesus also, that he might sanctify the people through his own
13 blood, suffered without the gate. Let us therefore go forth
14 unto him without the camp, bearing his reproach. For we have
not here an abiding city, but we seek after *the city* which is to
come.

### $13^{15, 16}$. *The nature of the Christian cultus.*

15 Through him then[2] let us offer up a sacrifice of praise to
God continually, that is, the fruit of lips which make confession
16 to his name. But to do good and to communicate forget not:
for with such sacrifices God is well pleased.

### $13^{17-25}$. *Concluding words.*

17 Obey them that have the rule over you, and submit *to them*:
for they watch in behalf of your souls, as they that shall give
account; that they may do this with joy, and not with [3]grief:
for this *were* unprofitable for you.
18 Pray for us: for we are persuaded that we have a good
19 conscience, desiring to live honestly in all things. And I exhort
*you* the more exceedingly to do this that I may be restored to
you the sooner.
20 Now the God of peace, who brought again from the dead the
great shepherd of the sheep [4]with the blood of the eternal
21 covenant, *even* our Lord Jesus, make you perfect in every
good [5]thing to do his will, working in [6]us that which is well-
pleasing in his sight, through Jesus Christ; to whom *be* the
glory [7]for ever and ever. Amen.
22 But I exhort you, brethren, bear with the word of exhorta-
23 tion: for I have written unto you in few words. Know ye that

[1] Gr. *through*.   [2] Some ancient authorities omit *then*.   [3] Gr. *groaning*.
[4] Or, *by* Gr. *in.*   [5] Many ancient authorities read *work*.   [6] Many
ancient authorities read *you*.   [7] Gr. *unto the ages of the ages.*

our brother Timothy hath been set at liberty; with whom, if he come shortly, I will see you.

24  Salute all them that have the rule over you, and all the saints. They of Italy salute you.

25  Grace be with you all. Amen.

# COMMENTARY

$1^{1-3}$. *Summary of the Christology of the Epistle.*

1–3. Opening statement of faith outlining some of the main ideas to be developed. 'Christ greater than the prophets' might constitute a sub-heading of the paragraph.

**1. 1.** The order of the Greek words throws the emphasis on *by divers portions and in divers manners*, methods of revelation which the writer contrasts in v. 2, with the complete and unified revelation in Christ. The present verse anticipates, in a remarkable way, the view of the Old Testament revelation which has been reached through scientific criticism, as a library of very various books recording 'words of God' delivered in many different periods of Jewish history.

Hebrews, though ending like a letter ($13^{23-25}$), lacks the regular epistolary beginning. Was it, as Dr. Scott suggests (see p. 15), a discourse written by an orator for some one to deliver on his behalf, rather than a letter? Perhaps the bearer was charged to improvise a greeting, the composer preferring to open straightway with this diapason note. Of one thing we can be sure—that the absence of the greeting is not due to any desire on the writer's part to remain unknown to his readers. Mutual acquaintance between writer and reader is implied throughout. See e.g. $13^{18.23}$.

2. *at the end of these days.* The words suggest at once the main point of the letter, the absolute finality of the revelation in Christ, cf. $9^{26}$, 'now at the end of the ages'.

*in his Son.* The Greek words say (as in R.V. margin) 'in a Son'. The qualification of sonship is thus contrasted with the qualification of mere prophethood. A son displays, not only by his words but in all that he is, his father's nature. Compare v. 3, 'the very image of his essence', and $12^{10}$ (with note).

*heir of all things.* All things will own Him as Lord. Compare $10^{13}$ 'From henceforth expecting till his enemies be made the footstool of his feet'.

*heir.* Is the parallelism between this passage and the parable of the husbandmen and vineyard (Mark $12^{1-10}$) merely accidental? In both cases a succession of prophets is followed by the arrival of 'the heir'. For another point of contact between this parable and Hebrews see note on $13^{12}$.

F

*through whom also he made.* The Son is the Alpha as well as the
Omega, the Beginning as well as the End (heir of all things).

It is not mere coincidence that the N.T. writings in which the
doctrine of Christ as God's Agent in Creation is developed (viz.
the Fourth Gospel, Colossians, and Hebrews) are those which are
aimed at an incipient Gnosticism. It was in fact probably
directly under the pressure of Gnostic tendencies that the belief
was arrived at. Gnosticism, which was in the field before
Christianity,[1] quickly adopted Jesus as one of the aeons or
angels which it proclaimed to have been the instruments of
Creation. Christians, jealous for the uniqueness of their Lord,
replied 'No. He is not a creative aeon, but the one and only instrument of creation.' Then at once the O.T. personification of the
creative Wisdom of God and the Philonic doctrine of the creative
Logos lay ready at hand for the development of this doctrine.[2]

Dr. Moffatt remarks:[3] 'The early Christian, who believed in
the lordship of Christ over the world, felt, as a modern would put
it, that the end must be implicit in the beginning, that the aim
and principle of the world must be essentially Christian.' The
comment is worth quoting as suggesting a possible line of defence
of the doctrine in the present day, but, just because it is so
modern, it is correspondingly unlikely to represent the process
of thought by which the doctrine was originally evolved.

*the worlds* (τοὺς αἰῶνας). Rather, as in margin, 'ages'. Such was
the meaning of the word in N.T. times, and time looms large in the
present context,—'of old time' and 'at the end of these days'.

3. *being the effulgence of his glory, and the very image of his
substance.* The Son is the radiance of the Father's glory; and
'he that hath seen the Son hath seen the Father', for the Son is
to the Father as the impress made by a seal is to the seal. The
phrases suggest the superiority of the Son over the prophets as
a medium of revelation. The Greek word (character), rendered
'very image', has been taken over into the English language, and
was commonly used for the impression made by a seal.

[1] The best discussion of early Gnosticism is still Lightfoot's essay on
'The Colossian Heresy', in his commentary on Colossians and Philemon.
[2] The author of Hebrews nowhere calls the Eternal Son the Logos, but
in view of the acquaintance with the works of Philo which he displays
(see Introd., pp. 14, 17) it is reasonable to assume some influence of the
Philonic Logos upon his conception of the cosmic, creative activity of
the Son of God.        [3] *Comm.*, p. 6.

*effulgence of glory.* The Greek words (ἀπαύγασμα δόξης) are found in Wisd. 7²⁵ ᶠ·. The Greek word translated 'substance' (ὑπόστασις) occurs also in 3¹⁴ and 11¹. Its literal meaning is 'that which stands under' or 'underlies', and in the present verse it signifies 'essence'. Cf. the use of it, for 'substance', in the LXX of Psalm 139¹⁶. In its other contexts in Hebrews it must be differently translated (see notes *ad loc.*).

*upholding all things.* 'Upholding', the Greek word (φέρων) suggests both sustaining and carrying towards the destined goal of development. Such is part of the creative activity of the Son, a 'creative evolution'.

*by the word of his power.* Creation by the divine spoken word characterizes the narrative of Gen. 1, cf. Ps. 33⁶. It is doubtful whether '*his* power' refers to the Son or to God the Father. Like the preceding verse, v. 3 describes the Son in three phases, pre-existent, in the flesh, and exalted. That the everlasting Son assumed our full humanity and 'when he had made purification of sins sat down on the right hand of the Majesty on high' is, in outline, the positive theological theme of the Epistle.

*when he had made purification, &c.* By His priestly life and death He attained to kingly status and authority. Compare the emphasis in the Epistle on Melchizedek, the priest-king (7¹), as a type of the Christ.

*purification of sins.* See Introd., p. 38.

*sat down on the right hand.* The imagery here used to indicate Christ's triumph is drawn from Ps. 110¹, of which psalm the author makes more constant use than of any other part of the Old Testament. Cf. also 1 Kings 2¹⁹.

*of the Majesty on high.* Cf. the similar periphrasis for God in 8¹. It was characteristic of the Judaism of the rabbis to use such phrases in place of direct naming of the Deity. In both its contexts in Hebrews this periphrasis mitigates slightly the anthropomorphism of 'on the right hand'.

## 1⁴⁻¹⁴. *The Eternal Son greater than angels.*

4. *having become.* The Son is represented as superior to the angels not only by virtue of His eternal Nature *but by virtue also of the days of His flesh.* In writing 'having become' the author is anticipating the argument of 2⁶⁻⁹ (see notes), where he shows that the ultimate destiny of humanity, upon which Jesus has already entered, is to be higher than the angels.

*as he hath inherited, &c.* In view of the verse which follows it would seem that the inherited name must be that of 'Son'. Does the author mean that the eternal Being of whom he is writing became 'Son' by the Incarnation ? Such a view would hardly be consistent with 5⁸— 'though he was Son yet learned he obedience by the things which he suffered'. 'Inherit' and its kindred words are favourite expressions with our writer, occurring nine times in the Epistle (see Introd., p. 48), and we often use our favourite words rather loosely and with many different shades of meaning. In the present verse 'inherit' implies simply—'He possesses by lawful right a more excellent name than they.' After all, we do, in a loose sense of the word, *inherit* the name of 'son'. The title which Christ acquires by virtue of His earthly life is not Son but High Priest. See 5¹⁰ and note.

5. We shall notice, in the course of the Epistle, into what a large number of Old Testament texts the author reads a reference to the Messiah. Underlying his quotations in these verses is, of course, the assumption that his readers recognize Jesus as Messiah (as even Jewish-Christian Gnostics did) and also that they acknowledge the passages quoted to be Messianic passages.

6. It has been questioned whether we should translate 'and again when he bringeth', or 'when he again bringeth', i.e. whether the reference is to the first or second advent of the Messiah. Comparison with 10⁵ suggests the former alternative. And for the writer's comparative lack of interest in the second Advent see Introd., pp. 43 ff. and note on 9²⁸. Probably this verse is a reference to the tradition of the worshipping angels at the Nativity, recorded in Luke 2¹³ ᶠ· The quotation is from the LXX of Deut. 32⁴³, which, it must be admitted, can be treated as a Messianic text only by a highly arbitrary kind of exegesis.

*firstborn.* Compare Rom. 8²⁹, where St. Paul describes Christ as 'the firstborn among many brethren'. ('Many sons' occurs in Heb. 2¹⁰.) Christ as our elder brother, who has already attained to the status to which we shall attain, is, as we shall see, one of the leading thoughts of our Epistle. Meanwhile 'firstborn' in the present verse goes fitly with 'heir' in v. 2, cf. 12²³ (with note). We may note also that the title is used in Ps. 89²⁷ (which the writer no doubt regarded as a Messianic text), and that Philo speaks of the Logos as 'first-begotten' (e.g. De Confus. Ling. 14).

7. The passage quoted (Ps. 104⁴) runs, in the Hebrew original, 'He maketh winds his messengers and flames of fire his ministers'. The imagination of the rabbis played, however, upon the passage, and accordingly we read in 2 Esdras 8²¹ ᶠ·, 'Before whom the

hosts of angels stand with trembling: at whose bidding they are changed to wind and fire.' This transmutability of angels into material elements is probably what our author read into the verse, inferring from it the inferiority of the angels to the 'eternal spirit' (9¹⁴ see note) of the Son.

8. The author of the passage here quoted (Ps. 45⁶ᶠ·) meant, in all probability, 'God is thy throne for ever and ever'; but the writer of the Epistle interprets him as addressing the Messiah as God, a meaning which the Greek of the psalm will easily bear.

9. The text quoted in this verse suggests a moral probation of the Messiah, and would therefore appeal to our author, who boldly views the human life of Christ in that light. Compare 2¹⁸, 5⁸, &c.

10–12. The writer ventures to interpret Ps. 102²⁵⁻²⁷ as applying to the Son, inasmuch as he believes the Son to be God's Agent in creation. With vv. 11 and 12 cf. 12²⁶ᶠ·

13. As a climax to his series of quotations the author gives a verse of the psalm (110) of which he is going to make much in his argument later on.

14. To the angels is assigned the lowly position of servants of the servants of God.

### 2¹⁻⁴. Interlude of warning and exhortation based on the preceding Section.

2. 1. It is the author's method, as at this point, after a theological paragraph to turn aside into a paragraph of exhortation. Nor are these hortatory passages mere interludes in his letter, the object of which was to exhort his readers to secure a firm grasp of the true faith in the face of heresy and of persecution.[1] The writer himself in 13²² describes the whole Epistle as a 'word of exhortation'.

*drift away.* More exactly 'be carried away', by a current.

2. *if the word spoken through angels proved stedfast.* The author for his own hortatory purposes plays upon his readers' regard for Judaism. The Jewish Law, he reminds them, was spoken through angels, those beings which he has proved to be so inferior to the Lord, through Whom (v. 3) the Christian revelation was spoken. Yet even that inferior revelation had such force that, under its regime, every sin whether of commission or of omission

---

[1] For evidence of persecution threatening the readers see 12³ ᶠ·, with notes.

(Gr. παράβασις καὶ παρακοή, R.V. 'transgression and disobedience') was justly recompensed. Much more ought we, then, to give earnest heed to our superior revelation.

*spoken through angels.* The Old Testament nowhere states that the Law was mediated through angels, but the tradition of which the writer here makes use is mentioned by Josephus, *Antiquities*, xv. 5. 3, and three times in the New Testament, see Acts 7[53] and Gal. 3[19].

3. *which having been, &c.* 'Which' is an inadequate rendering of a Greek word meaning 'inasmuch as'. 'Inasmuch as it was at the first spoken through the Lord.' It came to us, says the writer, all but directly from the Lord Himself. God has spoken unto us in His Son (1[2]).

The significance of this important verse in regard to questions of the date, authorship, and destination of the Epistle has been dealt with in the Introduction, pp. 10, 27 f.

4. The point of this verse is to emphasize the awful authority of 'the things that were heard'. More correct than 'gifts' is the marginal rendering, 'distributions'.

*according to his own will.* The words do not appear as very relevant to the author's point. We can best account for them by supposing that they are reminiscent of St. Paul's words in 1 Cor. 12[11]—'The Spirit dividing to each one severally even as he will', where 'even as he will' emphasizes, for the benefit of the conceited Corinthians, the fact that spiritual powers are dependent not on the merits of the Christian possessing them but on the will of God.

### 2[5-18]. *The Human Christ greater than angels.*

5. This verse is fully intelligible only as a contradiction of a Gnosticism which pictured the heavenly spheres as peopled and dominated by heavenly beings. Josephus tells us (*B. J.* ii. 8. 7) that every one initiated into the community of the Jewish-Gnostic Essenes took an oath to guard 'the names of the angels' (see Introd., pp. 22 ff.). The writer's bold declaration (see notes on v. 7) that the 'world to come' is destined to be subject to *humanity* would come as a message of release to many fear-haunted souls, in that era of 'failure of nerve', when a universal fatalism, stealing over the world, assigned the ultimate control of man's destiny to more or less sinister heavenly beings.

*whereof we speak.* This may have a general reference 'which is the theme of our letter'. But in 6[5] the author writes of Christians as those who have 'tasted the powers of the age to come'. It may be, then, that the writer is thinking of the 'powers' which he has just mentioned in $2^4$ as 'powers of the age to come', as phenomena of the heavenly world of spiritual Reality breaking through the order of this material world. The outpouring of the Holy Spirit together with 'powers' of vision, &c., is given an eschatological setting, in the 'age to come', in Joel $2^{28\,\mathrm{ff.}}$

6–8. The remarkably vague manner in which the quotation is introduced has parallels in Philo, e.g. *De Ebriet.*, 14. The writer's conception of the inspiration of the Old Testament renders him comparatively indifferent to the human agent through whom the word was given.

It is important to realize that the author of Hebrews does not treat these verses of Psalm 8 as referring to the Messiah but to man as such, and in this respect his treatment is true to the meaning of the writer of the psalm. But in another respect our author departs from the original significance of the psalm, which sets forth the dignity of man in his place in the world, viz. only a little lower than the angels, crowned with the glory and honour of being lord of all his fellow creatures. In Hebrews a different significance is attached to the words 'a little' (Gr. βραχύ τι). They are interpreted as meaning not 'a little in degree', but 'for a little while', and the psalm is understood as describing the destiny of man in two stages or phases, 'for a little while' (i.e. in this world) 'lower than the angels', and then (in the world to come) 'crowned with glory and honour' and with all things in subjection under his feet. From this interpretation, which the Greek of the psalm will undoubtedly bear, the writer argues that 'not unto angels' but unto man did God 'subject the world to come'.

8. Nothing is excepted from this subjection. Angels, therefore, so far from being rulers in the heavenly places are, in that sphere, lower than man.

*But now we see not, &c.* It is true that humanity has not yet entered upon this destiny.

9. But in Jesus we see human nature thus glorified.

9. A difficult verse because many different thoughts are condensed into it.

With the tradition of our Lord's Ascension in his mind the author writes that we can see this ultimate destiny of man already fulfilled in Jesus, who has trodden the whole road of human destiny in both its phases. For a little while He was lower than the angels, but, through the gate of death, He has now entered into the destined glory.

*because of the suffering of death crowned with glory.* For man (as for Jesus in His humanity) the way to glory is through suffering, a thought which is repeated in the next verse and which was very apposite to the circumstances of the readers in the shadow of persecution.¹ Both the order of the Greek words and the context provided by the following verse require that 'the suffering of death' should thus be understood as the cause of the glory not as the purpose of the humiliation.

*that by the grace of God, &c.* The Incarnation and the Death, Resurrection, Ascension, and Heavenly Session of the Incarnate combine together to make His death a source of universal blessing. The idea that the exaltation of Jesus to God's right hand, His entrance into the Holiest, is an essential part of the great priestly act of sacrifice by which He sanctifies humanity is characteristic of the thought of the author of Hebrews.

*for every man* (ὑπέρ). Not 'instead of' but 'on behalf of', for the benefit of every man.

In this paragraph of the Epistle we should note that it is highly characteristic of its author to represent Christ as superior to the angels not only by virtue of His eternal Nature as Son of God, but also by virtue of His humanity. See note on 1⁴.

10. *it became him* (cf. 7²⁶—'such a high priest became us'), i.e. it suited His Nature.

*for whom are all things, and through whom are all things, &c.* God is responsible for the goal towards which all things are moving, and for the process by which they are destined to move towards their goal. The goal set before the sons of God is glory (see the psalm quoted above, where to be 'crowned with glory' is postulated as the ultimate destiny of man). And for sons the way to glory is through suffering (see the argument in 12⁵⁻¹¹). Since God is responsible for this plan He fittingly caused the pioneer of man's salvation to tread the same path to glory, i.e. the path of suffering.

*for whom are all things.* Cf. Rom. 11³⁶. The Epistle to the Romans was probably known to the author of Hebrews (see Introd., p. 16). But some such words as these had possibly become a liturgical formula.

*many sons.* For 'many' see note on 9²⁸.

¹ Persecution: see 12³ ff. and notes.

*author* (Gr. ἀρχηγός): better, as in A.V., 'captain'. The primary meaning of the word is 'pioneer'. Jesus has blazed out the trail which we follow. Christ as our forerunner appears frequently in the Epistle.

*to make . . . perfect* (Gr. τελειῶσαι). This verb occurs nine times in the Epistle, and its cognate substantive once (see Introd., p. 48). The translation in the English versions is unfortunate. The word signifies simply *to complete a process*, and its use here means that Jesus became *fully qualified* as pioneer of man's salvation by undergoing experience of human sufferings, inasmuch as through suffering is the way to salvation (cf. 5⁸ and note). Thus He became a 'merciful' or 'sympathetic High Priest' (2¹⁷).

11. This verse reiterates, explicitly, what has been implied in the previous verse, namely, that men and the Pioneer of their salvation are alike sons of one Father.

*he that sanctifieth.* The phrase probably represents the author's conception of Christ as the Mediator of the New Covenant (12²⁴). In Exod. 19¹⁴ we read that Moses, as the mediator of the Old Covenant, 'sanctified the people'. 'Sanctified' appears again in 10¹⁰, 10¹⁴, and 10²⁹.

*he is not ashamed.* Cf. 11¹⁶, 'wherefore God is not ashamed to be called their God', with note.

The author's object in the quotations which follow is to find Old Testament texts which foreshadow the assumption of full humanity by the Messiah.

12. Psalm 22 (v. 22), which breathes the spirit of the suffering servant of Deutero-Isaiah, and the opening words of which were uttered by our Lord on the cross, is very naturally quoted here as a Messianic psalm.

13. The first of these quotations (from Isa. 8¹⁷) calls for comment. It is impossible to see any reason for our author's use of it, except as suggesting that in the days of His flesh Christ walked, as men are called upon to walk, by faith alone, that He was one with us in this great fundamental respect. Christ as the supreme example, and therefore the inspirer of human faith, is indeed one of the bold ideas of the Epistle. In 12² for example He is described as 'the pioneer of faith'.

14. *the children* are, of course, those referred to in the immediately preceding quotation, i.e., according to our author's interpretation of Isa. 8¹⁸, humanity. In connexion with this verse emphasizing, as it does, Christ's assumption of flesh and

blood we should remember that no form of Gnosticism could tolerate the idea that Christ partook of flesh and blood. To the Gnostic all matter was inherently evil. Christ's human body was therefore only the semblance of a body.

13³ (with note) should be read in connexion with this verse. Christ, says our author, in order to be really one with humanity assumed a body which was subject to death. But He turned the mortality of His human body to good account. For He died a death which avails to deliver His brethren from the fear of death.

*bring to nought* (Gr. καταργήσῃ, 'to render powerless'). In its description of the devil as 'him who has the power of death' the verse reminds us of Wisdom 2²⁴. The words 'that through death . . . that is the devil' are to be understood in the light of v. 15. By His death Christ delivers man from consciousness of guilt (this is to be the theme of the middle portion of the Epistle). It is consciousness of guilt that makes death terrible (compare 'The sting of death is sin', 1 Cor. 15⁵⁶). Thus Christ delivers men from the fear of death, and robs of his power the devil, who is wont to brandish death as a weapon of terror before the eyes of the guilty-hearted.

16. The verse introduces a short summary of the argument of the full humanity of Christ which has gone before.

*take hold* (Gr. ἐπιλαμβάνεται). This rather curious phrase and the words 'seed of Abraham' are due to the influence of Isa. 41⁸ ꜛ· 'But thou, Israel, . . . the seed of Abraham my friend: thou whom I have *taken hold of* from the ends of the earth.' Christ came to the rescue not of angels but of men, and therefore (v. 17) He took full human nature. We shall fail to understand the wording of these verses unless we remember that Jewish Gnostics regarded the Christ as having the nature of an angel. The fact that human nature is described in v. 16 as 'the seed of Abraham' is due to Isa. 41⁸ and to the writer's interest in God's promise to Abraham that in his seed all nations should be blessed (see 6¹⁷). It must not therefore be taken as an argument for a Jewish Christian church as the destination of the Epistle.

17. The emphasis in this verse is on the words 'merciful and faithful'. The human experience described in v. 18 has made Christ sympathetic and also faithful, i.e. an example of human faith.

*that he might be* (Gr. γένηται). Rather ' that he might *become* '.

*in things pertaining to God.* See note on 5$^1$.
*make propitiation.* See Introd., p. 34.

### 3$^{1-5}$.  *Christ greater than Moses.*

**3.** **1.** *Apostle and High Priest.* As Westcott (Com. *ad loc.*) suggests, these titles are probably due to the thought of Christ as greater than both Moses, the apostle or emissary of God, and Aaron His high priest.

*Jesus.* The frequency of the occurrence of our Lord's human name in this Epistle is almost a commonplace, and is consistent with the author's emphasis upon His humanity.

2. Modelled upon Num. 12$^7$—'My servant Moses . . . is faithful in all mine house.' *His house,* therefore, = God's house.

3. *For.* The verse gives the reason for 'considering Jesus'. With the *form* of this verse compare 1$^4$. The *meaning* of it is that Moses, being described in Num. 12$^7$ as 'in the house', is a part of the household, whereas Jesus, as God's Creative Agent, is the founder of the house, and therefore greater than any part of it.

4. Philo,[1] commenting on 'the house of God' in Gen. 28$^{17}$, interprets it as including the whole sensible universe; and the wording of the verse under consideration suggests that the writer of Hebrews adopted Philo's allegorization. Every house has a builder, and the builder of the Universe is God, whose Creative Agent (see 1$^2$) is Christ.

5. A new distinction between Christ and Moses. We have had the distinction between the Builder of a house and a part of the house, and we now have the distinction between a servant in the household and a son over the household. Both the distinctions originate from Num. 12$^7$, the first from the words 'in my house', the second from 'my *servant* Moses'.

*for a testimony of those things which were afterward to be spoken.* The words are a parenthesis. Moses is represented as a faithful *servant* and his main service was to witness to the things which were afterwards to be spoken by the Lord. (That the Law of Moses was a 'shadow of things to come' is stated in 10$^1$.) Thus there is a double emphasis on the relative inferiority of Moses, servant to the Son, and his service simply to testify to the coming Son.

[1] *De Somn.,* i. 32.

3<sup>6</sup>–4<sup>13</sup>. *Interlude of warning and exhortation based on the
preceding Section.*

6. The writer starts, from the thought of Christ's household,
a period of exhortation. 'We are Christ's household *if we remain
faithful.*' The readers had become timid and ashamed about a
faith in which they should have waxed bold and gloried. All the
emphasis in the verse is on the provisional clause introduced by
'if', which would be better translated 'provided that'.

7–11. By the quotation of Psalm 95 the author seeks to
amplify the warning implied in the conditional clause of v. 6. 3<sup>12</sup>–4<sup>13</sup>
drives home the warning of the psalm quoted.

12. *evil heart of unbelief.* The writer suggests (see also the
next verse) that the root of unbelief, of unresponsiveness to the
'heavenly calling' (3<sup>1</sup>), is moral evil.

*the living God* is one of the writer's favourite phrases. See
Introd., p. 48. It represents a distinct difference between our
writer's theology and Philo's Platonic conception of God, as pure
Being, which is almost a 'pale abstraction'. As commentary on
the author's idea of 'the living God' we may take 4<sup>12 f.</sup>, and the
second half of 11<sup>6</sup>.

13. The writer foreshadows what he is going to argue very
soon, viz. that the present time may be brought under the
'To-day' of the psalm.

*hardened by the deceitfulness of sin.* A remarkable description
of the manner in which successive sins, each one seemingly in-
significant, gradually produce a fatal hardening of the heart,
rendering it impervious to all spiritual influences.

14. Again, as in v. 6, he holds up the high privilege of Christians
with a conditional clause of warning—'*provided that* (Gr. ἐάνπερ)
we hold fast . . .'

*partakers of.* 'Partaking of' is a favourite idea with the writer
(see Introd., p. 49). As has already been remarked (see note on 1<sup>4</sup>)
a speaker or writer tends to use his favourite expressions a little
loosely and vaguely. The Greek (μέτοχοι τοῦ Χριστοῦ) may mean
either 'partakers of Christ' or 'partakers with Christ'. Whichever is
the correct translation, the author is probably looking back to v. 6,
and means that we are members of the household of which Christ is
the Head.

*confidence.* The word is ὑπόστασις, which has appeared, in the
sense of 'essence', in 1<sup>3</sup>. Here it can only possess its alternative
meaning, viz. in the words of Moffatt, 'what a man bases himself on

as he confronts the future'.[1] The word is used in this sense of 'hope' in the LXX of Ruth $1^{12}$. It is a little more than 'hope', a 'sure and certain hope' (cf. $11^1$, with note).

15. This verse goes closely with the preceding 'We have to hold fast during this critical "to-day" which presents us both with a hope and at the same time with a danger of failure'.

16. The warning in the words, 'as in the provocation', just quoted is a very serious warning. It reminds us of a case in which a whole people provoked God, and that after they had made such a good beginning, in their exodus from Egypt under the leader whom God had sent to deliver them.

17. Sin incurred, in this case, the wrath of God for forty years: and the carcases of the sinners fell in the desert. A deliberate piling up of suggestions of horror.

18. Disobedience brought the penalty of not entering into the rest of God.

19. They had left Egypt for the promised land, but a gloomy chapter of sin, disobedience, and unbelief ensued, and in the end they could not enter in.

4. 1. *a promise being left* (Gr. καταλειπομένης, 'a promise being left over'). The idea is worked out in vv. 6–9. For 'left over' cf. note on $10^{26}$. Notice the cautious and delicate way in which the possibility contemplated in this verse is expressed, in contrast to the strong language in which the warning from history has been described. In such subtleties the pastoral heart of the author reveals itself. (Cf. $6^9$ and note.)

2. The writer now proceeds to draw the parallel lines between the spiritual position of his readers and that of Israel in the wilderness. Like the Israelites they have had preached to them a message of good tidings (the promise of a rest). But, as the historic parallel shows, mere hearing, even of a divine promise, is not enough: the word of God has to meet and mix with faith in the hearer.

Probably the reading 'the word of hearing did not benefit, not having been mixed with faith in them that heard it' is to be preferred to that adopted in the R.V. The R.V. reading gives an almost impossibly clumsy sentence, in which 'hearing' is used in two very different senses—mere hearing in the one case and hearing and receiving in the other. 'Those who heard' would, if the R.V. reading is accepted, presumably be Joshua and Caleb. But these two were

[1] *Hebrews* (International Critical Commentary), p. 48 (note on $3^{14}$).

ignored in 3¹⁶. The alternative reading gives a sense very similar to the Parable of the Sower, where the harvest depends not merely on the quality of the seed of the word of God but also on the condition of the soil with which it is mixed.

3. *For* should be rather the discursive 'now'. 'Now, as a matter of spiritual experience, we who have believed know ourselves to be entering into rest.'

There is a contrast between 'we who have believed' (in v. 3) and 'not mixed with faith' (in v. 2). 'We who have faith' would better bring out the contrast which the Greek (οἱ πιστεύσαντες) suggests.

*even as he hath said . . . they shall not enter.* The emphasis is on 'they', and the underlying thought is that already indicated by 'left over' in v. 1. The promise of a rest was unappropriated by those to whom it was made, and, accordingly, we find that the promise has been 'left over' and is open to us. To this point the writer explicitly returns in v. 9. Meanwhile, with the words, 'although the works were finished . . .', he branches out into a new development of his idea of the promised rest. The divine rest, he says, was as really existent in the days of those Israelites as it is to-day. It existed indeed from the very foundation of the world.

The author is typically Alexandrian and thoroughly allegorical in his interpretation of 'the rest'. For him its meaning in Ps. 95 is not exhausted by reference to the conquest and settlement of Canaan (cf. 4⁸ and note). It was an invitation to share in the sabbath-rest of God. Cf. his treatment of the promise to Abraham in 6¹⁷ (see note *ad loc.*).

The point of the writer, in remarking that the rest was in existence from the very beginning, is to reinforce the warning to his readers which he is deriving from the psalm. 'The rest' which the psalm tells us was held out to the Israelites in the wilderness was not a rest which was to come into being at a future date but a real rest, in existence at that very time, a rest which God Himself was at that time enjoying and into which He invited those Israelites. Let us realize then that not even the present reality of the promised rest is a guarantee that those to whom it is offered will enter into it.

4. Gen. 2² is quoted in support of the statement at the end of v. 3.

5. The rest mentioned in the psalm is the same sabbath rest of God referred to in Gen. 2².

6. The writer infers from the words of the psalm '*they* shall not enter into my rest' that it was God's intention that some one should enter in.

7. As a sign that this was God's intention, witness the fact that in David's day, with the words '*To-day* if ye shall hear his voice, harden not your hearts', God defined a new period in which the rest was to be open and accessible.

*saying in David.* The LXX ascribes this psalm to David. The Hebrew does not.

8. It might have been supposed that the psalm referred simply to the fact that the Israelites who left Egypt were forbidden to enter Canaan. The author of Hebrews, however, infers that 'the rest' was not the occupation of the holy land. Otherwise God would not, in David, long after the conquest under Joshua, have opened up a new period of probation for entering into the rest. The verse is thus parenthetical. Its form—'If Joshua (Gr. Ἰησοῦς) had given them rest'—is due to the author's desire to hint at yet another demonstration of Christ's superiority to the various ministers of the Old Covenant, in this case Joshua.

The denial that any real divine rest was attained by the occupation of Palestine is characteristic of our writer, in whose view the religious soul is always a pilgrim, finding on earth no fatherland. See 11<sup>13, 16</sup>, 13<sup>14</sup>.

9. A verse which sums up what has gone before. 'So we see a sabbath-rest is left over and remaining for the people of God.'

10. The verse explains why the writer has called our rest a sabbath-rest. In saying that it is a ceasing from works the writer is probably thinking of something like St. Paul's contrast between the life of faith in Christ and the life of performing the works of the law.

The real sabbath-rest open to us is of course not cessation from all activity. It is cessation from feverish and futile activity. Those who do the will of God are fellow creators with Him; and they are entering more and more into an easy proficiency in well-doing. Our sabbath-rest is also the satisfaction of seeing that what we have done in accordance with the creative purposes of God is, in the words of the Creation story, 'very good'. It is the joy of having garners full of the fruits of our labour.

11. *Let us therefore give diligence.* Better, 'Let us therefore be zealous' (Gr. σπουδάσωμεν).

12. Here is a personification of the Word of God. Between the Philonic personification of the Word and the Christology of Hebrews there is a close parallelism (see note on 1²). It is therefore remarkable that this, the only explicit personification of the Word in the Epistle, is brought into no sort of relation to the author's conception of the Eternal Son. The truth is that in this verse the writer is simply borrowing straight from Wisdom 18¹⁵ ff. 'Thine all-powerful word leaped from heaven out of the royal throne, a stern warrior into the midst of the doomed land, bearing as a sharp sword thine unfeigned commandment. . . . And each, one thrown here half dead, another there, made manifest wherefore he was dying.'

None the less the verse has a clear affinity also with the thought of Philo, who describes the Word as sharp and cutting, as dividing and re-dividing everything into its smallest component parts (*Quis rerum divinarum haeres*, 26). An instructive difference appears, however, between Philo's idea and what our author makes of it. The cutting function of the Logos in Philo is a philosophical conception of what Moffatt describes as 'the principle of differentiation in the universe',[1] whereas the conception in Hebrews is entirely ethical.

*to the dividing of soul and spirit, &c.* The meaning required by the context is not so much dividing of soul and spirit as penetration into the innermost recesses of the soul. Has the writer been led away slightly from his own meaning by Philo's statements concerning the differentiating functions of the Logos?

13. *laid open.* The Greek word (τετραχηλισμένα) means literally 'seized by the throat', hence simply 'captured'. In order to obtain a meaning more suitable to our context it has been conjectured that the word (which is formed from τράχηλος = 'throat') means 'with head thrust back and throat laid bare'—to the stroke of the sword of the Word. 'Exposed' would be the best translation.

*manifest.* Compare also Wisd. 1⁶ ᶠ.

The force of the personification of the Word in vv.12 ᶠ. depends upon the fact that the writer has been deriving his grave warning from the word of God. 'No dead letter',[2] this word of God!

---

[1] *Op. cit.*, p. 55.         [2] Moffatt, *op. cit.*, p. 55.

## 4<sup>14</sup>–5<sup>10</sup>. *Beginning of the setting forth of Christ as High Priest.*

14. (Cf. 10<sup>23</sup>.) The writer states in his own characteristic terms the confession to which, as his warning has shown, we must be so careful to hold fast.

*high priest, who hath passed through the heavens.* The metaphor is obviously derived from the high priest passing through the veil into the Holiest. And see note on 7<sup>26</sup>.

15. To encourage his readers to hold fast he reminds them of the sympathy of their high priest, a feature of Christ's character which he has already depicted in 2<sup>17 f.</sup>. He now makes clearer what he means by his former words 'in all things made like unto his brethren'.

The words *'yet without sin'* stand in an emphatic position in the Greek, and are no mere afterthought. They are as essential an element in the encouragement which the writer is here seeking to give, as is the thought that He was subject to all our temptations. Compare 7<sup>26-28</sup>. 'Without sin' reminds us that he was *faithful* to God as well as *sympathetic* to man. See 2<sup>17</sup>.

Davidson [1] has admirably written, 'Even of sin a sinner is an ill judge; he will either regard it with undue abhorrence, or with mawkish sentiment, or with a callousness that comes of thinking it a matter of course among men.' This is indeed the implication of Hebrews 5<sup>2</sup>, where the word which is translated, in the R.V., 'bear gently' means to strike a happy mean in the matter of feeling (Gr. $\mu\epsilon\tau\rho\iota\sigma\pi\alpha\theta\epsilon\hat{\iota}\nu$) and where Westcott comments 'towards sinners he must have that calm, just feeling which neither exaggerates nor extenuates the offence'.

*without sin.* This is not the usual Greek word, $\mathring{\alpha}\nu\epsilon\nu=$'without', but $\chi\omega\rho\acute{\iota}s=$'apart from'; and Westcott suggests [2] that the author meant by the words not that Christ was sinless but that He endured all our temptations except those that result from sin indulged in the past. It is true enough that temptations of that kind constitute an important exception to the general rule laid down in the verse. But there is really nothing in the writer's language to show that he intended to make this exception, which is indeed dependent on a rather subtle psychology.

'Without' is used only four times in the whole of the New Testament, while $\chi\omega\rho\acute{\iota}s$, 'apart from', is used forty times, and in many of these cases its meaning is quite undistinguishable from that of $\mathring{\alpha}\nu\epsilon\nu$. It is so used several times in Hebrews, e.g. 7<sup>7, 20</sup>, 9<sup>7</sup>. Moreover, we may be sure that the author would not have allowed himself to

[1] *Hebrews*, p. 108.   [2] *Comm.*, pp. 108 f.

make his bold statement about the manifold temptations of Christ without adding an assertion that He was free from sin. Furthermore, certain verses which follow, notably 7$^{26, 27}$ (see notes), seem to depend upon some such assertion having been made.

16. 'Having such a sympathetic high priest we may boldly approach.' The word προσερχώμεθα is characteristic of our author, who uses it seven times, always in the sense of drawing near in worship (see Introd., pp. 47 f.). We may take courage from the thought that our needs are so thoroughly known and understood in the heavenly places. Christ's 'mercy' flows from His sympathy, His power to 'help in time of need' from His faithfulness; and both these qualities are bound up with those 'days of his flesh' in which He became our High Priest.

**5.** 1. For the present tenses of this and the following verses see Introd., pp. 29 f.

1. A high priest is taken from among men because his function is to represent men to God.

*in things pertaining to God* (τὰ πρὸς τὸν Θεόν). We have already met with this phrase in 2$^{17}$. It is derived ultimately from the LXX of Exod. 4$^{16}$. But it occurs in Rom. 15$^{17}$, and the similarity of Rom. 15$^{16 f.}$ to this passage in Hebrews is perhaps close enough to suggest that our author had St. Paul's words in mind. For other similarities to Romans in this Epistle see Introd., p. 16.

2 and 3 develop further the reason why a high priest must be taken from among men; and we may notice how in these verses the Christian writer imports into the relationship between priest and people an element far more personal and pastoral than was present in the Jewish sacerdotal system. Cf. note on 7$^{25}$.

2. *bear gently.* (See note on 4$^{15}$.) It is important to notice that in this verse 'being compassed about with infirmity' is made an essential qualification for high priesthood: it ensures, the writer says, the necessary quality of sympathy. In the following verse we read that, as a result of being compassed about with infirmity, the Jewish high priest was 'bound as for the people so for himself to offer for sins'. From these premises we should logically infer that, in the writer's view, Christ was bound to offer sacrifice, not indeed for sins in Himself (an idea which is precluded by 4$^{15}$ and 7$^{27}$), but 'for that he himself also was compassed with infirmity'. This inference is justified by v. 7 (see note), which describes the offering made by Christ on His own behalf, inasmuch as He also was compassed about with infirmity.

3. *so also for himself.* See the ceremonies performed by the high priest on his own behalf on the Day of Atonement, in Lev. 16[11] ff..

4. Not only must the high priest be taken from among men, he must also be called by God. The call of Aaron is in Exod. 28[1]. Of the verses which follow, vv. 5[f.] show that Christ possessed the second qualification (called of God), vv. 7–9 show that He possessed the first qualification (taken from among men).

5. *So Christ also, &c.* Better 'Accordingly, even the Christ glorified not himself'.

6. Here is quoted for the first time the verse (Ps. 110[4]) which contains God's calling of the Messiah to priesthood; it is a quotation of which the writer is going to make much.

7. This verse, together with the verse which follows, describes the offering which Christ made on His own behalf (see v. 3 and note).

*having offered up.* The Greek (προσενέγκας) is the same technical word as is used in v. 3 of the offering of the high priest's sacrifices for himself and for the people.

The sacrifice which Christ offered on His own behalf, inasmuch as He was 'compassed about with infirmity' (v. 2) was, appropriately, an offering of 'prayers and supplications with strong crying and tears'. This offering was accepted ('having been heard'). These prayers and supplications were acceptable to God for they were the result of 'godly fear'. The reference is clearly to Gethsemane. But of what is the author thinking as the object of Christ's 'godly fear'? He tells us that Christ prayed to him 'that was able to save him from death'. Death, then, was the object of Christ's fear. The thought in this verse goes beyond that of 2[14]. In the earlier passage we are told that *sinful* men are in bondage to the terror of death. In the present verse, it is implied that man as such, 'being compassed about with infirmity' (i.e. prone to temptation) has a 'godly fear' of death; for many forms of death, and none, we may imagine, more than that which Christ endured, present the most acute temptations to deny God and fall away from Him. We may compare the words in the Office for the Burial of the Dead in the Prayer Book: 'Suffer us not, at our last hour, for any pains of death to fall from Thee.' In death as in life Christ was the Pioneer of human faith, a faithful High Priest.

In two senses Christ was 'heard for his godly fear' and 'saved out of death', (1) in the fearlessness and faithfulness with which He was enabled to face it, from His prayers in Gethsemane onwards; and (2) in the Resurrection.

8. *though he was a Son, yet learned obedience by the things which he suffered*. The capital letter with which the Revised Version spells 'Son' is essential to the understanding of this verse. In 12<sup>7 ff.</sup> the author argues that it is of the essence of all human sonship to learn obedience through suffering. 'Though he was a son yet learned he obedience by the things which he suffered' would involve a contradiction of 12<sup>7 ff.</sup> The author means that though he was *the* Son of God, he yet 'learned obedience' in the human way. The absence of the definite article with 'Son' in the Greek is an echo of 1<sup>2</sup> (see note): 'though he was Son' is, therefore, the best translation. 'Learned obedience' is a phrase characteristic of the author's bold conception of Christ's humanity. The daring paradox of this verse 'the eternal Son of God learned obedience' is a summary of the Christology of the Epistle. Learning obedience has of course no implication of disobedience any more than 'becoming perfect' in the following verse implies any period of positive imperfection. The writer visualizes the earthly life of Christ as a process of doing God's will (see 10<sup>5-9</sup>). The new circumstances of each new day constitute a new call to obedience to the will of God. Thus did He, like us, learn obedience in new forms to the very day of His death, and thus was He at His death 'made perfect' in regard to this process.

For the 'obedience' of Christ cf. Rom. 5<sup>19</sup> and, more especially, Phil. 2<sup>8</sup>.

9. Commentators have pointed out how symmetrically this and the two preceding verses are arranged. Christ *learned obedience* to the God who was able to *save* Him and who *saved* Him. To those who *obey* Him Christ is the author of *salvation*. Note the parallels of 'obedience' and 'salvation'.

*author of salvation* (Gr. αἴτιος σωτηρίας) appears in Philo, *De Agricul.* 22.

*eternal salvation*. 'Eternal' is no mere decorative epithet. It introduces the theme of the Melchizedek priesthood of Christ which opens in the following verse, and the characteristic of which is priesthood 'for ever' (see e.g. 6<sup>20</sup>). And as the priesthood is 'for ever' so is the salvation which it mediates 'eternal', unlike such temporary salvations of the Old Covenant as had been achieved for instance by Joshua (see 4<sup>8</sup>). As commentary upon 'eternal salvation'

in the present verse see 7²⁴ ᶠ·—'He, because he abideth for ever, hath
his priesthood indissoluble, wherefore he is able to *save to the uttermost*
them that draw near to God through him'; and cf. 9¹² 'eternal redemption', with note.

10. *named of God.* Christ acquires this title and enters upon
the high priesthood which it represents through the completion
of the process ('having been made perfect', v. 9) which has been
described in the preceding verses. Having shown that Jesus
possessed the essential qualifications of priesthood the author
now goes on to indicate the order of His priesthood. But before
this theme is developed, in chapter 7, we have a digression, which
extends from 5¹¹ to the end of chapter 6.

5¹¹–6²⁰. *Digression to arouse the readers out of their dullness.*

11. The theme is to be abstruse and the writer doubts whether
his readers will be able to follow him.

12. *For.* Gr. καὶ γάρ, 'for indeed' or 'why!'.
*the oracles of God*, as in Rom. 3², the O.T. Scriptures.

12–14. The contrast between milk and solid food is to be found
in Epictetus (ii. 16. 39) and in Philo,[1] in two passages where the
parallelism to these verses in Hebrews is remarkably close. Philo
has the same words as Hebrews for 'babe' (νήπιος) and for the
'fully-grown' (τέλειος); the same word for 'food' (τροφή), the expression 'milky food' (cf. milk in Heb. 5¹² ᶠ·) and 'not partaking of'
(ἀμέτοχον) (cf. 'partaking of', Gr. μετέχων, in Heb. 5¹³). St. Paul
has (in 1 Cor. 3¹ ᶠ·) this distinction between the food of babes and the
food of the grown-up. Contrast the attitude of the simpler, less
intellectual St. Peter, in 1 Pet. 2², 'as new-born babes, long for the
spiritual milk'.

14. *exercised.* This verse, too straightforward to call for comment,
will help us to understand 12¹¹, where the same word (γεγυμνασμένα
='exercised') occurs.

**6.** 1. *let us pass on* (Gr. φερώμεθα). Rather 'let us be carried
on', i.e. by the argument.

*perfection.* Not, in this Epistle, moral perfection, but completion
of a process, in this case the process of instruction.

*of repentance from dead works, and of faith toward God*, has, at
first sight, a highly Pauline appearance. It must not, however,
be assumed that by 'dead works', even though in a Pauline
manner he contrasts them with faith, the author means 'works' in

---

[1] *De Migr. Abrah.* 6 and 9.

the Pauline sense. See the note on 9¹⁴. 'Dead works' in Hebrews means works which lack the living principle of faith. The reference here, as in 9¹⁴, is to evil works, i.e. sins. It is doubtful whether even St. Paul would have said that a man must *repent* of the works of the Law or that his conscience must be 'purged from them' (9¹⁴).

2. For 'baptisms' see Introd., p. 15.

For the importance of these verses (1 and 2) see Introd., p. 36.

3. The reference must be to 'pressing on unto perfection' (i.e. carrying on the instruction to its completion). See v. 1.

4. 'It is not worth while our going back' (see 'leaving' in v. 1) 'to discuss the elements of the faith, for it is impossible to renew again unto repentance those who have forsworn them.' For the rigorism of this paragraph see Introd., pp. 46 ff.

For 'enlightenment' as a term for conversion and the instruction which attended it cf. 10³². The word is not found elsewhere in the N.T. in this absolute form. In the present context it is specially forceful as a description of conversion, for it suggests the awfulness of 'sinning against the light'. Justin Martyr (*Apol.* lxi) writes 'This washing' (i.e. baptism) 'is called enlightenment' (or 'illumination'—Gr. φωτισμός), and from his day onwards the term becomes a common one for baptism.

Whether 'enlightenment' was borrowed in the first instance by Christianity from mystery religions must remain uncertain. But so much is said in both the Old and the New Testaments of the divine Light that the term may well have evolved naturally and spontaneously out of Christian experience.

*tasted of the heavenly gift.* Cf. 'tasted the good word of God' in v. 5. The metaphor of 'tasting' follows upon the analogy of feeding in 5¹²⁻¹⁴.

5. *powers of the age to come.* It is thoroughly characteristic of Hebrews to represent 'the powers of the age to come' as streaming down into this present age. See Introd., pp. 43 ff.

6. *crucify to themselves.* Is the author thinking of something more than moral backsliding, viz. of an apostate's deliberate denial of the faith, equivalent to a proclamation of Jesus as an impostor? Or does he merely mean that the sins of professing Christians cause Christ pain and bring reproach upon His name? The verse seems to indicate the only sense in which, in the author's view, Christ's sufferings can be repeated. (See 9²⁶ with note.)

7 f. Westcott calls attention to the influence of the phraseology of the Creation story upon these verses. With 'herbs' cf. Gen. 1¹¹; with 'thorns and thistles' cf. Gen. 3¹⁸. The blessing of God upon the herbs is in Gen. 1¹² and His curse is connected with the thorns and thistles in Gen. 3¹⁷ᶠ.

9. *beloved*: unique in this Epistle. Davidson remarks, 'Alarm at the awful suggestion of his own picture (vv. 4–8) causes a rush of affection into his heart'.

Mystery Religion. A youth, with veiled head, being initiated into the mysteries of Dionysius. Stucco decoration from the Villa Farnesiana

*things that accompany salvation* (Gr. ἐχόμενα σωτηρίας), or 'things connected with salvation', a similar vagueness to that of 'nigh unto a curse' in the preceding verse.

10. *God is not unrighteous* (Gr. ἄδικος). 'Righteousness' in the sense which is common in the Old Testament, where righteousness in God or in man is faithfulness to a covenant. 'God is not faithless' would be the best translation in the present context; alternatively 'God is not unjust'.

This is a remarkably un-Pauline verse, with its suggestion that the 'work' of the readers constitutes a claim on God. In 11⁶ belief in God as a *rewarder* of them that seek Him out is given as one of the axioms of faith.

The charity of the recipients of the Epistle commended in this verse probably has reference to the same events as are recorded in 10<sup>32-34</sup>.

*ministered unto the saints* (διακονήσαντες τοῖς ἁγίοις); cf. Rom. 15<sup>25</sup> (διακονῶν τοῖς ἁγίοις). The writer doubtless borrowed the phrase from St. Paul, but there is no necessity to suppose that he is referring to the Pauline collection from the Gentiles for the Christians at Jerusalem.

12. *sluggish* (Gr. νωθροί): the same word as, in 5<sup>11</sup>, is translated 'dull'.

*them who through faith and patience, &c.* The long roll of honour of these is to come in chapter 11; and in that chapter Abraham, of whom the author now proceeds, for a few verses, to discourse, is prominent.

13–20. The readers have good grounds for the faith and patience to which the writer has exhorted them in v. 12.

13. There is a close parallelism between this verse and Philo, *De Abrahamo*, 46, and *Leg. Alleg.* iii. 72. In the former passage Philo remarks that God took this oath 'for the sake of confirming Abraham's mind more steadfastly than ever before'. In the latter Philo says 'for you see God does not swear by another, for there is nothing greater than he, but he swears by himself, who is best of all'. He is, of course, commenting on the same text, Gen. 22<sup>16 f.</sup>, as Hebrews.

14. Gen. 22<sup>16 f.</sup>, 'By myself have I sworn, saith the Lord, . . . that in blessing I will bless thee. . . .'

15. *And thus* . . .: i.e. by virtue of God's promise, made doubly sure by God's oath by Himself, Abraham was able patiently to endure. Abraham is thus brought directly under the category of those mentioned in v. 12 'who through faith and patience inherit the promises'. Twenty-five years elapsed between the first fore-shadowing of the promise, referred to in v. 14, and the beginning of its fulfilment in the birth of Isaac. Cf. Gen. 12<sup>2, 4</sup> with Gen. 21<sup>5</sup>.

16. By universal human custom an oath is a very solemn and weighty matter. Witness the facts that (1) men swear by some-thing greater than themselves, and (2) such an oath is regarded as conclusive security in any dispute.

The reference in the first part of the verse is back to v. 13. God could not swear by anything greater than Himself.

The reference in the second half of the verse is forward to v. 17.

17. God adapted Himself to the human habit of mind which regards an oath as conclusive security. So far did He go in encouraging Abraham's faith and enabling him to endure.

*unto the heirs of the promise.* These words mark a transition in the application of the promise quoted in v. 14, from Abraham to the Christian readers of the Epistle, a transition which becomes more marked in vv. 18 ff.

The promise quoted in v. 14 is treated as having a double signifi- cance (cf. the author's treatment of the 'rest' in Psalm 95. See note on 4[3]). (1) It was the promise of the birth of Isaac. This was the promise which Abraham by patient endurance obtained (v. 15). (2) There was in the promise (in Gen. 22[18] 'in thy seed shall all the nations of the earth be blessed') a Messianic ele- ment, applicable to days far distant from the time of Abraham. Of this promise, fulfilled in Christ, Christians are 'the heirs'. This Messianic promise, to which even the saints of the Old Covenant never attained, appears again as 'the promises' in 11[13], and 'the promise' in 11[39]; where it stands contrasted with minor 'promises' (such as the birth of Isaac) referred to in 11[33]. See note on 11[13].

18. *two immutable things,* i.e. God's promise and His oath.

*we may have a strong encouragement.* Reading into the promise to Abraham more than the reference to the birth of Isaac, viz. Messianic implications, the writer presents it (together with its accompanying oath) as a ground of encouragement to Christians. 'We', he says, 'have the same security and certainty as enabled Abraham to endure with patience.'

The more probable meaning of the second half of this verse is 'that we who have fled for refuge (οἱ καταφυγόντες) may have a strong encouragement to lay hold of the hope set before us'. Philo (*De Profugis,* 15) similarly describes religion as 'the flight for refuge' (ἡ καταφυγή) 'to Reality'. Translated as above, v. 18 suggests —what we know to be true—that with some persons religion never advances beyond the negative stage of flight from the vicissitudes of worldly life, never attaining to firm apprehension of positive realities which rise above the changes and chances of our mortal life. It is a mere 'fleeing for refuge'.

19. It is impossible to say how far the simile of the anchor should be extended in the translation of this verse. Do the words 'sure and steadfast' &c. refer to anchor (A.V.) or to hope (R.V.)? The sense is the same in either case. Christian hope anchors us to the eternal world of heavenly realities, so that, though we may be storm-tossed, we do not drift and make shipwreck.

19–20. The Christian hope is fixed on things unseen (of the reality of which faith furnishes the conviction, 11[1]), a world veiled

from human sight. But through that veil, into that unseen world
Jesus has already passed, and, inasmuch as He 'was in all things
like unto us' (2¹⁷), His passage into that world is a pledge of our
passage into it. He has passed in, then, as our 'forerunner'.
This is the surest ground of Christian hope, a ground more secure
than even Abraham possessed, an even greater incentive to
'patient endurance' (v. 15) than was his.

*the veil* (καταπέτασμα) is the inner veil, dividing the Holy from the
Most Holy Place. The outer veil was in Greek κάλυμμα.

20. With the thought of Jesus passing through the veil we
return to the thought of His high priesthood, from which the
digression started in 5¹⁰. The concluding words of 5¹⁰ are here
repeated; and we are now about to hear concerning Melchizedek
those 'many things hard to be interpreted' (5¹¹). So orderly is the
writer of the Epistle even in his very digressions.

### 7¹⁻³. *The meaning of Christ's Priesthood after the Order of Melchizedek.*

**7. 1.** *For.* The following words give the reasons why Christ's
priesthood was 'after the order of Melchizedek'.

The author makes such a collection of the scanty details about
Melchizedek given in Gen. 14 as will furnish him with a mystical
or allegorical interpretation of them.

*blessed him*: the significance of this is discussed in v. 7.

**2.** *to whom also Abraham divided a tenth part.* This is discussed
in vv. 4–6, 8–10.

*King of righteousness* is, of course, an interpretation of the
word 'Melchizedek'. In this verse the writer probably had in
mind Ps. 85¹⁰, 'Righteousness and peace have kissed each other',
a psalm which undoubtedly looked forward to the Golden or
Messianic Age, and which would therefore help both the writer
and his readers to see in Melchizedek, King of Righteousness and
King of Peace, a Messianic significance.

**3.** Gen. 14¹⁸⁻²⁰ refers neither to the descent, birth, nor death of
Melchizedek, who both appears and vanishes suddenly and
mysteriously in the scene of history. The Alexandrian method
of exegesis, seeking for a double meaning in every line of Scripture,
finds its very silences charged with significance. From the silence
of Gen. 14 as to the origin and ending of Melchizedek, it is here
inferred that he is a 'type' of the eternal Son of God.

*made like unto*, i.e. in the pages of Scripture, which thus represent him as a 'type' of the Messiah.

*abideth a priest continually.* The words of Psalm 110, 'a priest
for ever after the order of Melchizedek', are read by the writer of
Hebrews into the silence of Gen. 14 as to Melchizedek's death.

(What the writer of Psalm 110 meant by the Melchizedek priesthood is a different question. He wrote, probably, in honour of Simon
Maccabaeus who, like Melchizedek, combined the functions of ruler
and priest.)

### 7⁴⁻¹⁰. *The Melchizedek priesthood greater than the Levitical.*

4. *Abraham, the patriarch.* The order of the words represents the
emphatic position in which 'the patriarch' stands in the Greek.

5. *they of the sons of Levi that receive the priest's office*, i.e. only
those sons of Levi who were descended from Aaron. By the Law
the Levitical priesthood is placed in the privileged position of
taking tithes of descendants of Abraham.

6. What, then, must be the privilege vested in one who, though
not of Levitical descent, took tithes of the patriarch Abraham
himself!

9, 10. This, to us, strangely expressed idea is guarded by the
qualifying phrase 'so to say' (Gr. ὡς ἔπος εἰπεῖν). 'We might
almost say that in the person of their ancestor the Levites may be
regarded as having paid tithes to Melchizedek.'

### 7¹¹⁻²⁵. *The Melchizedek priesthood supersedes the Levitical and the Law inextricably bound up with the Levitical priesthood.*

11. 'Perfection' (τελείωσις), cf. 7¹⁹. For the explanation of the
word in this context reference must be made to 9⁹. See note.

In Psalm 110, so runs the argument of the verse, God promised
another priesthood. This promise implies that the old Aaronic
priesthood was inadequate.. It was upon the old priesthood that
the old law, given under that priesthood, depended.

12. A new priesthood means a new law.

13. The new priest (after the order of Melchizedek) whose
advent is heralded in the psalm comes not from the tribe of Levi;
and by the old Law all tribes other than Levi were excluded
from priestly service at the altar. Therefore the Law is abrogated.

14. As a matter of well-known historical fact Jesus (whom we
all recognize as Messiah and therefore as the priest to whom the
psalm refers) came of the tribe of Judah. His priesthood makes,

then, a clean breach in the Mosaic Law, which allows no priesthood to the tribe of Judah. Though the writer says nothing of
the Davidic descent of our Lord, he seems certain of His descent
from the royal tribe.

15. *And what we say is yet more abundantly evident*, i.e. our
contention for the superiority of the Melchizedek priesthood to
the Levitical and for the consequent annulling of the Levitical
Law.

*after the likeness.* Cf. 'made like unto' in v. 3.   See note.

16. *carnal.* More than one derogatory idea is associated with
the word in this context: (1) The Law provided for a priesthood
by *physical* descent. (2) Those who exercised priesthood under the
old Law were *mortal* men.   (3) The Law which instituted the
Levitical priesthood was a law concerned primarily with *externals*.
(See 'carnal ordinances' in 9¹⁰.)   Perhaps the mortality of the
Levitical priesthood is the main point which the author here in-
tends (as in v. 8 and in vv. 23 f.) to contrast with the eternity of
the Melchizedek priest.

*endless* is inadequate (Gr. ἀκαταλύτου).   'Indissoluble' (R.V. margin)
is better.

18, 19. Summary of the preceding argument, to the effect that
the new priesthood involves the disannulling of the old Law.

*For* should be, more properly, the argumentative 'now'.

19. *the law made nothing perfect.* This theme, here a mere
parenthesis, is to be developed in 10¹⁻⁴.   In the present context
it suggests the reason for that abolition of the Law which the
author is engaged in proving.

*a bringing in thereupon* (Gr. ἐπεισαγωγή), more definitely 'a substitution'.   As Dr. Moffatt points out, it is used by Josephus of the
substitution of Esther for Vashti (*Ant.* xi. 6. 2).

*Draw nigh* (Gr. ἐγγίζομεν).   Here is the author's favourite
idea of religion as the approach of the worshipper to God, expressed this time by a different word from his usual προσέρχομαι,
which is, however, coming very shortly, in v. 25.

20–2. In these verses the curiously great importance which the
writer attaches to oaths (see 6¹³, ¹⁸⁻²⁰) again shows itself.   So far
does this tendency in him go that he declares that we can measure
the superiority of the covenant which Jesus mediates by the fact
that He (unlike the Levitical priests) is, in Scripture, proclaimed
priest with an oath.

23. The old priesthood was continually changing hands because of the mortality of those who exercised it.

24. *unchangeable*. The translation fails to reproduce the force of the Greek word (ἀπαράβατον) which is a legal term for 'inviolable'. Christ's priesthood is inviolable by the one power which can violate priesthood, viz. death. The translation 'that doth not pass to another' (see R.V. margin), though it would fit the context, is not admissible, being an active rendering of a passive word.

25. Into this verse has crept from the pastoral spirit of Christianity the thought of something more than the purely official relationship between priest and worshipper which obtained in Judaism. (Cf. note on 5², ³.) The changes which death entailed in the personnel of the Jewish priesthood could not really have mattered to the worshippers who 'drew near to God' through their ministrations. Jewish priests were functionaries in a system. Their relation to the worshippers was entirely impersonal. But the author is none the less right in remarking on the preciousness to Christians of the unchanging and unfailing nature of their Priest, 'the same', as he says elsewhere (13⁸), 'yesterday, to-day, and for ever'.

The author sets out to interpret Jesus in terms of the Levitical priesthood, but the terms are not quite adequate to the Subject, Who transforms the idea of priesthood in the process, infusing into it a pastoral element which the Jew found, if anywhere, rather in his rabbi than in a priest.

*able to save to the uttermost*. Salvation 'to the uttermost' may be the long process of a lifetime, but we shall never find that our needs have outlived our Priest and His power to meet them.

*to make intercession for them*. For Christ's work of intercession cf. Rom. 8³⁴. In describing the activity of the living Christ in relation to the human soul the author is influenced and to some extent limited by the analogy of the Jewish priesthood. That is, no doubt, the main reason why he describes that activity as intercession. But it should be noted that this function of intercession with which Christ is here invested was by some orthodox Jewish writers, and no doubt by Jewish Gnostics, assigned to angels. See Job 33²³ ᶠ·, Dan. 12¹. In the Testament of Levi, 3⁵, angels are described as 'ministering and interceding with the Lord for all the ignorances of the righteous'.

Experience shows us that two of the most necessary qualifications for fully effective intercession are: (1) a vivid realization of

the needs of those on whose behalf intercession is made ; (2) the
fullest possible self-devotion of the intercessor to the cause for
which he intercedes. Hebrews brings into prominence Christ's
possession of both these qualifications. The first of them is emphasized in such passages as 2¹⁷ᶠ·, 4¹⁵ ; the second in the picture
of our Lord's entry upon His work of intercession, His passing
through the veil with the offering of His own life-blood, shed for
those for whom He intercedes (9¹², ²⁴⁻²⁶, &c.).

### 7²⁶⁻²⁸. *Our need of such an eternal High Priest.*

26. In the words of this verse are summed up the qualities of
the ideal High Priest.

*became us* (Gr. ἡμῖν ἔπρεπεν). Cf. 2¹⁰, i.e. 'suited our nature',
'was what we needed'.

*separated from among sinners.* The phrase suggests both the points
which are explicit in 4¹⁵ : 'in all points tempted like as we are, yet
without sin'. 'Compassed about with infirmity' like sinners, yet
'separate from them' in His holiness.

*made higher than the heavens*, i.e. exalted 'into heaven itself now
to appear before the face of God for us' (9²⁴). The 'heavens' of
which the writer is thinking in the present verse are those
material heavens of which he writes, in 12²⁶⁻²⁷, that they are
to be 'shaken' and pass away. Cf. 'passed *through* the heavens'
in 4¹⁴.

27. Another feature of the general superiority of Christ's priesthood to the Levitical, viz. that His offering was of such infinite
value that it did not need to be repeated—a theme which is
introduced and re-introduced in subsequent passages of the
Epistle. The argument in this verse is comparable to the similar
contrast between 'one' and 'many' in 7²³ ᶠ·. One priest, one
offering, the author considers to be an obviously superior system
to many priests, many offerings.

The writer here confuses the daily offerings of the Jewish
priests with the annual offering of the high priest on the Day of
Atonement, but the confusion hardly affects his point.

*for this he did.* The thought at this point is very condensed.
But the following are obviously the two leading ideas: (1) That
Christ did not need to offer for sins of His own at all (see 4¹⁵ and
note on 5²), and (2) for the sin of the people He needed to offer only
once. Such was the nature of His offering that (1) it could not

be repeated, for it was the offering of Himself and (2) it availed 'once for all' (Gr. ἐφάπαξ, cf. Rom. $6^{10}$), for the same reason, viz. that it was nothing less than the offering of Himself. Inasmuch as it entailed His death, its repetition was impossible. Inasmuch as it was so precious an offering, its repetition was unnecessary. Cf. note on $9^{26}$.

28. An even more condensed verse than the preceding. Its purpose is to establish the point mentioned in v. 27, viz. that Christ's offering was so precious as to avail once for all, not needing to be repeated. A sacrifice, in the writer's view, depends for its value upon two things : (1) the qualifications of the priest ; (2) the nature of the offering. Whereas in the case of the Law the priests were ordinary sinful men, in the case of Christ's offering the sacrificing Priest was the Son of God Himself, fully qualified ('perfected'), further, by His human life to be the Priest of humankind. Not only was this the exalted nature of the Priest of our great sacrifice, but it was the nature also of His offering, inasmuch as this was the offering of Himself. Into this complex of ideas the author has drawn three additional thoughts : (1) of Christ's priesthood being established by an oath (cf. $7^{20-22}$) ; (2) of that oath as having superseded the Law (cf. $7^{11\ \text{ff.}}$) ; and (3) of that oath as having proclaimed Christ a priest 'for evermore' (cf. $7^{21-24}$).

$8^{1-5}$. *The Tabernacle in which our High Priest ministers.*

**8.** 1. *Now in the things which we are saying the chief point is ...* See R.V., but 'chief point' is rather a weak translation of κεφάλαιον which, like κεφαλή, is frequently used in the sense of 'crown' or 'completion'. In the preceding verses the writer has been outlining the characteristics of the High Priest which our nature requires, and in this verse he continues 'Now the crown and completion of what we are saying is the fact that *we have* such a High Priest'.[1]

2. In this verse a new branch of the topic of Christ's priesthood, viz. the sanctuary in which He ministers, is opened up, and it is at this point that the author's idealist philosophy comes fully into play. This philosophy has already been apparent in the general assumptions underlying the argument, the existence of a spiritual world, which is the real world, beyond and above the appearances

[1] I am indebted to my friend the Very Rev. H. N. Bate, Rector of Hadleigh and Dean of Bocking, for guiding me in the correct interpretation of this verse.

of earthly life, the world into which Christ has passed as the forerunner (6²⁰), a world to which the hope which Jesus inspires anchors the Christian soul (6¹⁹), a world the spiritual forces of which have been released by Christ for the believer, and even now stream down upon him (6⁵, ⁷ᶠ·), a world of which we shall read in the great eleventh chapter as the heavenly city towards which all faithful souls make pilgrimage. All this is much more idealistic, in the philosophic sense, than were the conventional eschatological modes of thought inherited by Christians from the Jewish apocalyptists. But in the present verse we reach a more specific, more concrete, and (if the paradox may be permitted) more realistic piece of idealism, the conception of a spiritual sanctuary, a 'greater and more perfect tabernacle, not made with hands, that is to say, not of this created order' (9¹¹), of which the old, visible sanctuary was a manufactured copy. This greater sanctuary the writer declares to be the sphere of Christ's priestly ministry. Into it He passed by His priestly death.

In the verses which now follow we see the process by which the author arrives at his conception of the heavenly tabernacle. It is by way of Exodus 25⁴⁰, a verse from which he deduces not only the existence of a spiritual sanctuary, but also the relative inferiority of the Jewish Tabernacle which was only an earthly copy of the heavenly.

3. This verse is a parenthesis and should be placed between brackets. A sanctuary is for the author essentially a place of sacrifice; and the statement, in v. 2, that Christ has a sanctuary in which He ministers, leads him to remark that Christ has an offering which He ministers, for the 'having of somewhat to offer' to God is the very essence of priesthood. The theme of the nature of Christ's offering, already anticipated in 7²⁷ ᶠ· (see notes), is to be developed later, in 9¹¹–10¹⁴. Meanwhile we return to the heavenly sanctuary.

4. This verse follows on vv. 1, 2. The sphere of Christ's priesthood must be elsewhere than on earth, for the exercise of priesthood on earth was given by the Law exclusively to others than Jesus, viz. to priests from the tribe of Levi (see 7¹²⁻¹⁴ and notes).

5. The inferiority of the ministry of these Levitical priests is here deduced from the inferiority of the sanctuary in which they ministered. For further comment on this verse see note on 8² and Introd., p. 42.

*Shadow.* Cf. 10¹ with note.

113

**6.** *he hath obtained.* Note that here and throughout the Epistle Christ is said to have *become* Priest by virtue of the manner in which He lived His human life. Cf. $5^{1\,ff.}$ and notes on $1^4$ and $2^{17}$.

The verse sets forth the superiority of Christ's priesthood to the Levitical in yet another aspect, viz. the superiority of the Covenant which it mediated. The worship of God by Israel is conceived in the Old Testament as based upon a covenant-relationship, that is to say, upon certain terms laid down by God as conditions by conformity with which access to Him can be obtained. Thus a covenant, as the present verse implies, is constituted by divine promises, promises that the worship of God shall be within the reach of those who fulfil the conditions laid down in the covenant. Jesus, says the writer, is the mediator of a new covenant enacted upon better promises than those of the Old Covenant. He is the mediator of this new covenant not only as the spokesman of its promises but as having by His life and death made possible a new and closer worshipping relationship of man with God.

The use of 'mediator' in connexion with covenant-making is natural. God on the one hand and the people on the other are regarded as negotiating parties and there is an intermediary between them. Cf. Gal. $3^{19}$ and Heb. $9^{15}$ and $12^{24}$.

**7.** We may speak freely of a better covenant and better promises because it is clear that the Old Covenant was not perfect. Otherwise there would have been no need that God should promise to those who were living under the Old Covenant (in the passage, Jeremiah $31^{31\text{-}34}$, which follows) a new covenant.

*no place would have been sought.* For this rather curious mode of expression cf. $12^{17}$, 'he found no place of repentance though he sought for it'. It is one of the author's mannerisms.

**8.** *finding fault* corresponds with 'faultless' in the preceding verse.

*with them,* i.e. with those who were living under the Old Covenant, which had failed to 'make them perfect' ($7^{11,\,19}$, $9^9$. See notes *ad loc.*).

**10.** *And I will be to them a God,*
    *And they shall be to me a people.*
A description of the nature of the Covenant relationship, the very

essence of which is, in the mind of the author of Hebrews, a worshipping relationship of a people with their God.

12. To this verse of the passage quoted from Jeremiah the writer attaches, as will appear, the greatest importance. It begins with 'for'; and indeed the whole of what precedes it in the quotation depends upon it. Forgiveness of sins is the essential prerequisite of the knowing and worshipping of God, i.e. of covenant-relationship (see note on $8^6$ and Introd., pp. 38 f.). In the ninth and tenth chapters the writer, in attempting to show that Christ is the mediator of a better covenant, argues that Christ has really made possible that forgiveness of sins which is the necessary first element in a covenant-relationship. He attempts to show, on the other hand, what the promise in Jeremiah implies, that under the Old Covenant this forgiveness of sins was not attained. Meanwhile in v. 13 he remarks again that the promise in Jeremiah of a new covenant implied that the former covenant was becoming outdated and outworn, and indeed like all such things was soon to disappear. For the bearing of this verse on date of the Epistle, see Introd., p. 29.

### $9^{1-10}$. *Futility of the sacrifices under the Old Covenant.*

**9.** 1. *even* is omitted in several MSS. If correct, it must mean 'even though transient'.

*of this world* (Gr. κοσμικόν). The translation in the text is supported by the use of the same word in Tit. $2^{12}$, and by its emphatic position in the present verse; for throughout this section of the Epistle the writer's emphasis is on the comparative earthliness and materialism of the sanctuary of the Old Covenant.

Other translations have been suggested: (1) 'Public'. Josephus (*Bell. Jud.* iv. 5. 2) uses the word in this sense, of the services of the Jewish Temple. But it would be difficult to see any appropriateness in emphasizing in the present context the publicity of the Jewish sanctuary.

(2) 'A symbol of the Kosmos or universe'. The thought of the Jewish Temple as such a symbol appears in both Philo (*Vit. Mos.* iii. 3–10) and Josephus (*Ant.* iii. 7. 7). But such an idea would stand unrelated to anything else in the present context.

(3) 'Ornamented'. It is true that the writer goes on in the next verse to describe the ornaments of the tabernacle, and that the noun for which the adjective in question is derived sometimes

means 'ornament'. But there seems to be no other instance of the adjective being used in this sense.

2. The catalogue of some of the furniture of the Tabernacle which follows is, as the author suggests in v. 5, of no significance for the argument of the Epistle. The author does not appear to see any mystical significance in these objects in detail. Perhaps they are mentioned to emphasize the comparative materialism of the Old Covenant. Note that his enumeration of them does not suggest that his readers were devotees of orthodox Judaism, familiar with the apparatus of its cultus, but rather the contrary.

7. *which he offereth for himself, and for the ignorances* (marg.) *of the people.* This double offering, which has already been mentioned in 5³ and 7²⁷, is a marked feature of the ceremonial of the Day of Atonement in Lev. 16.

*ignorances* (marg.) is correct. See Introd., p. 46.

8. The only detail of the Jewish sanctuary into which the writer cares to read a divine meaning is the veiling of the Most Holy Place.

For the bearing of this verse on the date of the Epistle see the Introd., p. 29.

9. *a parable for the time now present.* In the Greek words (εἰς τὸν καιρὸν τὸν ἐνεστηκότα) there is probably a double significance, (1) a parable which was to last until the time now present, i.e. until the new dispensation of Christ, and (2) a parable of which we Christians can now see the symbolic meaning, i.e. a parable instituted *with a view to* the time now present, when its significance would become clear.

*gifts and sacrifices*, as in 8³; but in 8⁴ 'gifts' is used to cover every kind of offering, including sacrifices.

*make the worshipper perfect.* 'Perfect' and 'perfection' are not, as we have seen, used in this Epistle of absolute moral perfection, but only relatively to some process implied in the context. 'The sacrifices of the Law could not touch the conscience, and therefore made no adequate provision for true worship.' For it is an axiom of the Epistle that you cannot worship with a guilty conscience. See Introd., pp. 38 ff.

10. The reason for their ineffectiveness. 'They were purely external ordinances' (Greek 'ordinances of flesh'). And then, feeling that he has perhaps attached too little significance to them, the writer adds that they had a temporary value. They were 'imposed until a time of reformation', presumably as a 'parable' (cf. v. 9) of the need of cleansing. Cf. 10³ and note.

The interpolation in this verse of the reference to 'meats and drinks and divers washings' is significant. 'Meats and drinks and washings' cannot be regarded as a particularly appropriate description of the 'bodily ordinances' of the Jewish Law. On the other hand, the words are an apt description of the 'bodily ordinances' of Gnostic asceticism; and the writer's object is to suggest that the heretical practices to which his readers tended had just the same ineffectiveness for the conscience, and consequently for worship, as the Jewish sacrifices.

$9^{11}$–$10^{18}$. *The efficacy of the sacrifice of our High Priest contrasted with the old sacrifices.*

11. *having come* (Gr. παραγενόμενος). Better 'having come on the scene', for the word suggests the interposition of an entirely new phenomenon. We have arrived now at the description of the 'time of reformation' mentioned in v. 10.

*good things to come* (Gr. τῶν μελλόντων). If this be the correct reading, the significance is of course eschatological. A rather less well-attested reading is τῶν γενομένων, 'the good things which came' through Him.

12. *his own blood.* See Introd., pp. 34 ff.

*entered in once for all.* (Cf. note on $10^{12}$, 'sat down for ever'.) This is not exactly congruent with $9^{28}$, on which see note.

*eternal redemption*, i.e. His redeeming act needed not to be repeated. The N.T. metaphors of ransom and redemption applied to the work of Christ have given rise to notorious strange and profitless speculations. It has often been asked, for example, to whom the ransom or redemption was paid. To God or to the devil? The writers who applied the metaphor show no signs of pressing it so far. The value of it for them, and for us, lies in the suggestion that the work not only means everything to us but also cost not a little to the 'Redeemer'. See further, Introd., pp. 31 ff.

13. In order to obtain in v. 14 one of his *a fortiori* arguments, the author here envisages the possibility of assigning to the Jewish sacrifices a certain positive, though limited, value (as distinct from the rather negative value with which he credits them in $10^3$). 'Purely external ordinances', he says, 'perhaps avail for the removal of purely external ceremonial uncleanness. If so, how much more. . . .' The mere removal of ceremonial uncleanness was the avowed object of some of the Levitical ceremonies, as, for example,

the ritual of 'the ashes of a heifer' (described in Num. 19). But the Jews looked, of course, for much more than this from (e.g.) 'the blood of goats' on the Day of Atonement. It is doubtful, however, how far they would have admitted the rigid distinction which is drawn in these two verses between ceremonial and moral uncleanness.

14. Four elements of superiority in Christ's offering: (1) It was the life-blood of Christ Himself. (2) It was a self-offering, conscious and willing, unlike the offerings of animals. (3) Though it was an offering consummated by death, it was the offering of an indissoluble life. (4) It was an offering without moral blemish, whereas the offered animals were merely without physical blemish.

The third element indicated above is the meaning which we must probably attach to 'through eternal spirit'. (The Greek words lack the definite article.) We should expect in this verse, which seeks to estimate the value of the Victim of the Christian Sacrifice, a reference to His eternal nature, of which so much is made in connexion with the efficacy of His priestly Ministry elsewhere in the Epistle (most notably in $7^{15\,f.}$). The words 'through an eternal spirit' are probably synonymous with 'after the power of an indissoluble life' in $7^{16}$. 'Through' is used vaguely, as in vv. 11 $^{f.}$, to denote a particular characteristic of Christ's offering.

It must, however, be admitted that the Greek word πνεῦμα (even without the definite article) often represents in the pages of the N.T. the Holy Spirit. If the R.V. is correct in inserting the article in this verse, the meaning will be that Christ's offering of Himself was in accordance and in co-operation with the Will of God, as revealed by the Holy Ghost in the pages of Scripture. Cf. $9^8$ where the Holy Ghost is expressly mentioned as the Agent of revelation in the writing of the Old Testament, and $10^{5-10}$ where the author finds in a psalm a prediction of Christ's offering of Himself.

14. *dead works*. The ceremony of sprinkling the ashes of a heifer, referred to in the previous verse, was for the cleansing of those who had incurred defilement through contact with a dead body. It is no doubt this fact which determines the use of the phrase 'dead works' in this context, and the meaning is 'defiling' works, i.e. sins. Cf. 'dead works' in $6^1$, with note.

*to serve*. The Greek word (λατρεύειν) is frequent in the Epistle (see Introd., p. 48), and signifies serving or worshipping in a sanctuary. In $9^9$ it is the word which the R.V. translates 'the worshipper'. We have, therefore, in the present verse, the author's characteristic contention that Christ's sacrifice by cleansing our conscience makes it possible for us to worship.

*the living God*. A favourite phrase in the Epistle. See Introd., p. 48.

15. *And for this cause he is* . . . . Because (see note on $8^{12}$) cleansing of conscience, forgiveness of sins, is the basis of the covenant-relationship.

*mediator*: cf. note on $8^6$.

*that a death* . . . Underlying the words is the axiom, explicit in v. 22, that for the forgiveness of sins a death is necessary. The death which inaugurated the New Covenant was also, the author states, retrospective, with a bearing upon the Old Covenant as well as the New. What did it effect in regard to the Old Covenant? It achieved forgiveness for the sins committed under the Old Covenant. Some such statement is almost demanded from the writer in view of his reiteration of the powerlessness of the ordinances of the Old Covenant to effect forgiveness of sins. In the minds of those who had read such verses as $9^9$ would arise the question, 'Were, then, all those of the Old Covenant left in their sins?' The answer of the present verse is that such of them as had been called were redeemed by the death of Christ, and by virtue of that death received and realized the promise which had been held out to them, viz. the promise of an eternal inheritance. The verse thus anticipates the great roll-call of the saints of the Old Covenant in chap. 11. 'Called' in the present verse corresponds with the calling of Abraham in $11^8$. Abraham was 'called' to receive an inheritance; and in $11^{9\,f.,\,13-16}$ the patriarchs are described as looking for an eternal inheritance. (Possibly in 'called' in this absolute form there is also a Pauline influence. See e.g. Rom. $8^{30}$.) In the eleventh chapter, as in the present verse, the saints of the Old Covenant are regarded as not having, in their own lifetime, received the promise ($11^{13}$) but as having been kept waiting until the Christian dispensation ($11^{39-40}$). The manner in which Christ's death affected the faithful departed the writer of Hebrews does not attempt to describe to us. But cf. 1 Pet. $3^{18-20}$.

16–17. For the space of two verses the author plays on the double meaning of the Greek word (διαθήκη) for 'covenant', which in the course of the first century of our era became the regular term for a 'last will and testament'. Upon this fact the author seizes in his desire to show the full fitness of the death of Christ.

17. *where there hath been death.* Note R.V. marg.: Gr. 'over the dead'. A rather strange turn of phrase, literally 'over corpses'. Possibly the writer desires to combine for the moment the two meanings of 'testament' and 'covenant', and is influenced by the recollection of such customs of covenant-making over dead bodies as are described in Gen. 15$^{9\text{-}18}$ or Jer. 34$^{18\text{-}20}$. In such ceremonies it is probable that the death of the animals symbolized the death which the covenanting parties invoked upon themselves, if they should break their covenant. The oath, so familiar in the Old Testament, 'the Lord do so to me and more also' is a covenant-making oath, intelligible only in connexion with the killing and cutting up of the animals in the Covenant ceremony. 'The Lord do to me as I have done to these animals and more also.' That this particular ritual of covenant-making 'over corpses' was a widespread custom is suggested by the fact that the Hebrew word for to '*make* a covenant' is really to '*cut* a covenant'. Covenant-making thus involved a death and was done 'over corpses'. The main thought, however, in these verses of Hebrews is obviously of a will and testament.

Is there possibly in Luke 22$^{29}$ a similar play on the testamentary meaning of the Greek verb from which 'Covenant' is derived: 'and I (who am about to die) bequeath ($\delta\iota\alpha\tau\iota\theta\epsilon\mu\alpha\iota$) to you a kingdom even as my Father has caused me (His Son) to inherit it' ($\delta\iota\epsilon\theta\epsilon\tau o$)?

18. We return to the pure and simple '*covenant*' sense of $\delta\iota\alpha\theta\eta\kappa\eta$. The author demonstrates from the ceremonial attending the institution of the first Covenant the appropriateness of the New Covenant being inaugurated by a death. His object, however, is not to remove the 'stumbling-block of the cross of Christ', but to set forth the self-sacrificed Jesus as the mediator of a New Covenant.

19. The details of 'water, scarlet wool, and hyssop' will be found in the ceremonial for the cleansing of a leper in Leviticus 14, though not in the account of the institution of the Covenant in Exod. 24. The author is quoting from memory and does not remember very accurately. Cf. the inaccuracies in 7$^{27}$ and 9$^{20,\ 21}$ (with notes). One is tempted to speculate that if he had been writing to Hebrews he might have been more careful to be accurate about the details of the Jewish cultus.

*Hyssop.* Several stems of hyssop (probably the caper plant) were bound together to constitute a sprinkler.

20. *This is the blood.* In the LXX, as in the Hebrew, of Exod. 24[8] Moses is recorded to have said '*Behold* the blood'. The slight change of the words in the present verse is probably due to unconscious reminiscence on the author's part of our Lord's

THE CAPER PLANT

words (Mark 14[24]), 'This is my blood of the covenant', a text very pertinent to much of the covenant speculation of Hebrews.

Nothing is said in the O.T. of Moses sprinkling *the book* on this occasion.

21. Here is an inaccuracy more remarkable than those already noticed. The tabernacle was not in existence at the time of the institution of the Covenant in Exod. 24[8]. In Exod. 40[9], however, Moses is commanded to anoint the tabernacle and all its contents with oil. The deviations from O.T. history in vv. 19–21 are more probably due simply to defective memory (cf. 12[21] note) than to any alternative rabbinic tradition. We should note, however,

that (in *Ant.* iii. 8. 6) Josephus describes Moses as smearing the tabernacle and its contents with blood as well as oil. On the Day of Atonement blood was smeared by the High Priest upon the 'mercy seat' (Lev. $16^{14}$) and upon the horns of the altar (Lev. $16^{18}$). The purpose of this proceeding is expressly stated— 'to make atonement for' the holy place and the tent of meeting (Lev. $16^{16, 20}$). This, had the writer remembered accurately, would have been sufficient to establish his point, in v. 22, that according to the law it is blood-shedding that has the power of cleansing.

22. For comment on this verse in its bearing on the destination of the Epistle, see Introd., pp. 25 f.

23. Judged with prosaic literalness this verse contains the extra-ordinary statement that the heavenly realities, of which the taber-nacle and its apparatus were material copies, needed cleansing. The material tabernacle was regarded as defiled by the sins of the people in whose midst it was pitched (Lev. $16^{16}$), but it is hardly probable that the writer of Hebrews was thinking of the contamination of human sin as extending to 'the greater and more perfect tabernacle'. 'Purified' in the present verse must be connected with 'dedicated' in $10^{20}$. The writer is almost prepared to say that the entry of Christ into the heavenly places consecrated them to be a sanctuary, a place of offering. It would be foolish to draw logical deductions from what is obviously a forced parallelism. Nor should we (in spite of this verse and $8^5$) assume that the author felt himself to be committed to the belief that all the details of the Israelite sanctuary corresponded to heavenly counterparts. His hasty and indifferent manner of enumerating them, in $9^{2-5}$, suggests the contrary. The general principle of material things as symbols of the spiritual both appealed to him and suited his present argument, but he was too large-minded to care to apply it in detail (cf. $9^5$, 'of which things we cannot now speak severally').

*copies.* See $8^5$.

24. The writer in this and the two verses which follow is harping again on his frequent theme, the superiority of Christ's priestly offering as exemplified by (*a*) the sphere in which it is ministered (v. 24), (*b*) its absolute, eternal value, calling for no repetition (vv. 25–26).

26. It is of the very essence of the nature of Christ's offering— the ultimate surrender of a human life—to be single and un-repeatable. (We may say that Christ's self-sacrifice is too com-plete and final an act ever to be repeated. He gave all that He had.) The idea of His having often suffered since the foundation

of the world, in the author's judgement, needs only to be men-tioned to appear as self-evidently grotesque. But see $6^6$, with note.

*at the end of the ages.* Cf. $1^2$, 'at the end of these days'. In the present context the thought of the End is suggested partly by the counter-phrase 'the foundation of the world', but much more by the conviction of the finality and absoluteness of the Christian Revelation which inspires this whole paragraph of the Epistle (cf. $1^2$ and note).

*put away sin.* See Introd., p. 38.

27. Certain Gnostics who, like all Gnostics, sat lightly to the doctrine of the humanity of Jesus, contemplated a whole series of incarnations of the aeon Christ. Any such idea is rejected as un-thinkable in $9^{26}$ (see note), and in the present verse the writer gives the reason why it is unthinkable. It is because of the reality of and completeness of Christ's humanity. 'It behoved him in all things to be made like unto his brethren' ($2^{17}$); and 'it is appointed unto men *once* to die'. Man can only once make the complete offering of his life in death. Beyond that he cannot go. It is his 'full, perfect, and sufficient sacrifice'.

*and after this judgement.* The thought of judgement (which here follows immediately upon death) emphasizes still further the finality which the author has in view, for judgement is passed upon a life as a whole when its completion has been attained. In this verse death is mentioned as if it were part of the natural lot of man. There is indeed nothing in the Epistle to suggest that physical death is essentially connected with sin, an idea common in St. Paul's writings. In $2^{14 \, f.}$ we are told that the *fear of* death is due to sin, a very different proposition.

28. Again the author embarks on a somewhat forced paral-lelism. The first parallelism is valid enough. 'As men die, so Christ died *once.*' But the solemn words that follow—'after this the judgement'—have no appropriateness to the life and death of Christ. And yet, says the writer, Christ too is concerned on the other side of the grave with judgement—as Judge. It is, accordingly, of Christ's return in judgement that the writer goes on to speak. Only it is upon the bright aspect of the picture that he dwells—upon what Christ's appearing will mean to those who look for Him. Thus the argument moves away from strict parallelism to the 'judgement' in the second half of v. 27. The words of v. 27 have a sinister tone, from the oppressiveness of which

we are rescued by the rather unexpected happy ending of v. 28. No words in this verse contribute more to its general tone of reassurance than 'without sin' ($\chi\omega\rho\grave{\iota}s$ $\dot{a}\mu a\rho\tau\acute{\iota}as$ as in $4^{15}$, see note).

Connecting 'without sin' with 'once offered' we find a phrase remarkably similar to Rom. $6^{10}$, 'in that he died, he died unto sin once'. There can be little doubt that reminiscence of the Pauline passage has influenced the rather curious wording of the verse in Hebrews, and that the meaning is the same in both epistles, emphasizing the joyful and triumphant fact that Christ's dying for sins is over and done with once for all. Cf. the connexion between Rom. $6^{10}$ and Heb. $7^{27}$ (see note).

The whole sentence 'shall appear a second time without sin unto salvation' is suggestive of the reappearing of the Jewish High Priest on the Day of Atonement. The 'congregation' had watched him as he made his way through the veil to that mysterious Most Holy Place, of which he alone knew the secrets. They waited eagerly for his reappearing, the sign of sin removed, of atonement consummated. Thus Ben Sirach writes, in Ecclus. $50^{5 \text{ ff.}}$, of Simon, son of Onias, the high priest—'How glorious was he when the people gathered round him At his coming forth out of the house of the veil! As the morning star in the midst of a cloud, As the moon at the full: As the sun shining forth upon the temple of the Most High, And as the rainbow giving light in clouds of glory.'

For further comment on the 'reappearing of Christ' in this verse see Introd., p. 44.

*to bear the sins of many*, see Introd., p. 35. The use of 'many' in this context (cf. Mark $10^{45}$) is a legacy to the N.T. from Isa. $53^{11-12}$. Cf. 'many sons' in $2^{10}$.

**10. 1.** *the good things to come.* Interpretation of this verse must start from these words, which have occurred already in $9^{11}$. Even for the Christian the good things of God are still largely 'good things to come'. From the standpoint of this Epistle the Christian looks both backward and forward. He looks backward upon those of the Old Covenant, so far behind the vantage-point at which he finds himself in Christ, upon those who 'saw and greeted' only 'from afar' the promises which he has received ($11^{13}$). But he looks forward also. The very faith by which he lives is defined ($11^1$) as 'the conviction of things *hoped for*'. Though brought by Christ into a perfect worshipping relationship with God, he has not yet attained to all the fullness of knowledge and power which are to come. He has 'tasted the powers of the age to come' (6$^5$), but that age is nevertheless an 'age to come'. It is 'within the veil' (6$^{19}$). Here he has 'no abiding city' but 'seeks one to come' (13$^{14}$).

Thus at the opening of this tenth chapter three phases are indicated: (1) a shadow of the good things to come (the past, represented by the Jewish Law); (2) the very image of the good things to come (i.e. the present revelation: Christ and all that He means to the world); (3) the good things which are to come hereafter. Thus the use of 'very image' (Gr. τὴν εἰκόνα) in this verse refers to the revelation of heavenly realities in Christ, and is parallel to Col. 1$^{15}$ where St. Paul describes Christ as 'the very image' (Gr. εἰκών) 'of the invisible God'.

The contrast between 'shadow' and 'image' is less common in Greek than that between 'shadow' and 'substance' or 'body' (Gr. σῶμα). The latter is found in Col. 2$^{17}$—'Feast-day, new-moon or sabbath, which things are a shadow of the things to come, but the *substance* (σῶμα) is Christ's', a verse so closely parallel to Heb. 10$^1$ as to imply literary connexion between the two.

*continually* (εἰς τὸ διηνεκές, as in 7$^3$, 10$^{12, 14}$). A similar phrase to that translated 'to the uttermost' (Gr. εἰς τὸ παντελές) in 7$^{25}$. In both verses occur also the words 'them that draw nigh'.

*make perfect*: as before in this Epistle, in relation to the process contemplated in the context; in this case the process of 'drawing nigh' or approaching God in worship.

2. Compare the complementary statement in v. 18; and see Introd., pp. 38 ff. Are we to take this verse as implying that the Christian once converted and baptized has never any more 'conscience of sins'? St. John is startlingly explicit (1 John 3$^9$)—'Whosoever is born of God . . . cannot sin because he is born of God.'

3. *remembrance* (Gr. ἀνάμνησις). The same word as in 1 Cor. 11$^{24-25}$, 'This do in remembrance of me'. Here, perhaps, as in 9$^{20}$,[1] is a reminiscence of the tradition of our Lord's words at the Institution of the Eucharist. In the Christian equivalent of the Jewish sacrifices (see 13$^{10, 11, 16}$ and notes *ad loc.*) is celebrated a joyful remembrance of our Redeemer from sin. In the Jewish sacrifices themselves there can have been nothing but a painful remembrance of the fact of sin, constantly reinforced with every

[1] See note *ad loc.*

repetition of the sacrifices. Thus, though he does not develop the theme, the writer might have described the Jewish sacrifices as St. Paul described the Law—'our tutor to bring us unto Christ'. The author of Hebrews nowhere suggests the Pauline idea that it was the function of the Law to make 'sin exceeding sinful'. To him it is always a medium through which men might see the shadow of the Truth (e.g. in the present context *the need* of cleansing from sins). The difference between the attitudes of the two writers towards Judaism may, perhaps, be stated thus: that Hebrews depicts the Law as a mild pedagogue *leading* men to Christ, while with St. Paul it is a stern pedagogue *driving* men to Him. Nevertheless when dealing in Colossians (2¹⁷) with a heresy similar to that refuted in Hebrews St. Paul similarly describes the Jewish Law as the shadow of the reality of which the substance is in Christ. See note on 10¹ above.

The clue to the difference between St. Paul's conception of the Jewish Law and that of Hebrews is to be found in the fact that whereas the Law in St. Paul's epistles means the ethical precepts, in this Epistle it means the ceremonial enactments. In Gal. 3¹⁹ St. Paul writes, 'What then is the law? It was added because of transgressions.' He means that it was given to deepen and increase the sense of sin, and consequently the sense of the need of redemption. This it did by setting an impossibly high standard of conduct, impossible because the Law which set it gave no aid by which to attain to it.

Hebrews too might have stated that the Law was 'added because of transgressions'; but in the different sense that, as a 'shadow of the good things that were coming' in Christ, it symbolized not only the need but the nature of the coming redemption. Neither writer allows that the Law has any saving power, but whereas St. Paul assigns to it only the function of bringing home by its commandments to sinful humanity the desperateness of their condition, Hebrews regards it as foreshadowing also by its ceremonial system the hope of future salvation.

*year by year.* Cf. 9²⁵. He is thinking of the sacrifices of the annual Day of Atonement, when every devout Jew made a solemn recollection of his own sins and when the sins of the whole people were ceremonially confessed by the High Priest (Lev. 16²¹).

4. As in 9²⁶ (see note *ad loc.*), the writer considers that the idea

has only to be stated baldly for its inherent absurdity to become at once apparent.

5. *when he cometh into the world he saith*. The author, very finely, takes the words quoted in this and the following verses as the key-note of Christ's ministry and life from the beginning to the end.

*a body didst thou prepare me*. So the LXX. The Hebrew of Ps. 40[6] has 'ears hast thou digged for me', i.e. 'the capacity for hearing Thy voice hast Thou given to me'.

6. Similar depreciation of the value of animal sacrifices (so pertinent to our author's purpose at this point) appears also in Ps. 50[8 ff.], 51[16].

7. *In the roll of the book*. The Psalmist meant, of course, the Law. The spirit of the Psalmist is indeed consonant with Jesus' summary of the Law, in Mark 12[28-31]. The word translated 'roll' (κεφαλίς) means literally 'little head'. Its use in connexion with 'book' in the LXX has been variously explained as derived from 'chapter-heading' or the top of the stick round which the papyrus was rolled.

8-9. The author's beloved method of pointing out that the Old Testament itself contains indications of its own ultimate supersession by a loftier faith. In the present context its application is specially appropriate, inasmuch as the psalmist in question truly saw a higher duty than animal-sacrifice, and Jesus, while not condemning the sacrificial system, so taught and so lived that its observances became, for His followers, inept.

10. *By which will* (Gr. '*In* the which will'), i.e. the will of God referred to in the psalm and carried into effect by Christ.

The writer concentrates upon the death of Christ as the supreme moment of Christ's performance of the will of God. The world of sacrificial metaphor in which his thoughts are moving dictates this concentration, as does also the reference, in the quotation with which he is dealing, to the '*body* prepared' by God. Nevertheless, the writer in this passage reaches out towards a wider vision of the nature of the offering which Christ made to God. That offering consisted, he suggests, in His complete self-dedication from beginning (v. 5) to end (v. 10) to the will of God. The spirit of this paragraph is enshrined in Du Bose's memorable phrase—'Jesus' single consistent, life-long, cross-completed act'. Compare also St. Bernard's 'Non mors sed voluntas placuit sponte morientis'.

The language of this verse is not now outdated. The complete self-sacrifice of Jesus in the doing of God's will still constitutes the main source of the world's sanctification.

*we have been sanctified.* Commentators on St. Paul have taught us that in the Pauline writings Sanctification is a gradual process of which the beginning is Justification. St. Paul thinks of our first conversion to Christ largely in forensic terms. In 'Hebrews', where religion is conceived as worship, the beginning of the new life is described as sanctification, on the analogy of rites of purification preliminary to worship. (See Introd., p. 38, also 2^11 and 10^14, 22 with notes *ad loc.*) The thought underlying the present verse is best interpreted by reference to Exod. 24^8, already referred to in 9^20 (see note).

11. A vivid picture of the futility which the writer sees in the continual offering of unconscious animal victims.

12. The dignity of Christ's effectiveness is in sharp contrast to the preceding verse. The contrast is gained largely by the juxtaposition of 'day by day', 'the same', 'can never', in the one verse with 'one sacrifice for ever' in the other. It is heightened by the contrast between the strenuous daily *standing* of the priest in v. 11 and the calm majesty of the *session* at the right hand of God in v. 12.

The Greek of the verse is such as to make it possible to connect 'for ever' with 'sat down', instead of with 'one sacrifice'. This interpretation is probably to be accepted as making a still more striking contrast between standing daily and sitting down for ever. Cf. 'entered once for all' in 9^12. The language in which Christ's triumph is described, in vv. 12–13, is of course determined by the psalm (110) which looms so large in this Epistle.

14. He can sit down and 'expect', for His work is done. The writer here deduces the finality of Christ's achievement from the wording of the 'Messianic' psalm 110, v. 1.

*perfected,* as elsewhere in this Epistle = 'put into a perfect worshipping relationship'.

*them that are sanctified.* The Greek tense is no longer (as in v. 10) past. Probably 'the sanctified' is the best rendering (so Moffatt). But the present tense may indicate a more Pauline conception of sanctification (see note on v. 10). Absolute precision in such terminology was (even if it be desirable) not achieved in the apostolic age.

15 ff. represent an attempt of the writer to deduce the finality of the Christian revelation from Jer. 31^31-34, a passage from which,

in $8^{8 \text{ ff.}}$, he has already inferred the divine intention to supersede the old covenant. Assuming that his readers are willing to identify Christianity with Jeremiah's New Covenant he calls their attention to one of the features of that covenant—'their sins and their iniquities will I remember no more'. Continuation of sacrifice is therefore (v. 18), in a serious sense of the word, inappropriate.

17. There is a lacuna in the Greek of this verse. The gap must be filled by reference to v. 15. 'After he had said, This is the covenant . . . He also said, And their sins and their iniquities I will remember no more.' The author so eagerly hurries on to the words of v. 17 which supply his main point, the very basis of covenant-relationship, that he forgets to supply the grammatical connecting link. This is a frequent habit with St. Paul, but a unique phenomenon in Hebrews. See Introd., p. 10.

18. Is complementary to the statement in v. 2.

### $10^{19\text{-}25}$. *Exhortation based on preceding sections.*

19 ff. As in other parts of the Epistle a theological paragraph is followed by a paragraph of spiritual exhortation; as a basis for which the author gathers up (in v. 19) his previous arguments.

19. *boldness* (Gr. παρρησία). Cf. $3^6$, $4^{16}$, $10^{35}$. Failure to realize the absoluteness of their Faith, the completeness of their Christian privileges, was the root of their difficulties. The frequency of the word for 'boldness' in the New Testament indicates the sense of emancipation from various fears and repressions which was and is one of the greatest blessings of Christianity (cf. note on $2^5$). The thought of this 'boldness' is expanded a little in v. 22 (see note *ad loc.*).

*to enter into the holy place.* The idea of our entering into the holy place has not previously been expressed in the Epistle, though the germ of it is in $6^{19}$ and $9^8$, as also in the constant emphasis on the fact that our Forerunner or Pioneer has entered into the Holiest. In pictorial metaphor it presents the writer's characteristic idea of religion as a perfect worshipping relationship; and it starts in the author's mind two new trains of thought, (1) The abolition of the veil which hitherto shut off the Holiest (v. 20), (2) the priesthood of all believers (v. 22; see note *ad loc.*).

20. Cf. 'The way into the holy place' ($9^8$). As it was opened up for us by the passing before of our High Priest, it is appropriately described as being 'dedicated' by Him. The author conceives of

it as dedicated or consecrated by His blood. Cf. $9^{18}$. For a still bolder expression of the idea contained in this verse, see $9^{23}$ and note.

*living.* 'Living God' is a favourite phrase of the author (see Introd., pp. 48.), and in $4^{12}$ we have the 'living word' of God. 'Living' is an epithet freely used in the New Testament (e.g. 'living stone' in 1 Pet. $2^4$). The freshness and spiritual vitality of early Christianity are suggested by the manner in which the Way [1] is described in this verse.

*that is to say, his flesh.* Westcott (*Comm.*, pp. 322 f.) suggests that these words are to be connected not with 'the veil' but with 'the way'. The way for us Christians through the veil into the eternal world of spiritual realities is the way of Christ's flesh, i.e. the same way as He took 'in the days of His flesh' ($5^7$): an attractive interpretation and well in keeping with the importance which is attached in Hebrews to Christ's humanity and His example. A more common and straightforward interpretation connects 'that is to say, his flesh' with the words which immediately precede it, representing Christ's flesh as the veil through which He passed into the Holiest. This symbolism becomes intelligible if we remember the tradition preserved in the Synoptic Gospels of the rending, at the moment of our Lord's death, of the veil which shrouded the Holiest in the Jewish Temple. From the freedom of access into the Holiest, of which he writes in v. 19, the writer naturally passes to the thought of the abolition of the forbidding veil. How was the veil abolished? By the death of Christ. His sacrificial death was His passing through the veil. The death of His body was the rending of the veil.

St. Luke ($23^{45}$) represents the rending of the veil of the Temple as having occurred before our Lord's death at some time during the darkness which covered the earth for three hours during the crucifixion. It is St. Matthew and St. Mark who state that it synchronized with our Lord's death; a fact which tells slightly against Lucan authorship of Hebrews. See Introd., p. 10.

21. The verse is intended to carry back the readers to the thoughts of $3^{1\text{-}6}$. As in $3^1$ (see note *ad loc.*) Christ's combination of the functions of Aaron (the priest) and Moses ('faithful in all God's house', Num. $12^7$) was perhaps in the writer's mind.

22. *let us draw near.* Once more, 'draw near in *worship*'. This

[1] The Way appears to have been one of the earliest names for the Christian Faith as a whole. See Acts $9^2$, $19^9$, $19^{23}$, $24^{22}$.

verse in fact resumes the theme of v. 19—'boldness to enter into the holy place'. 'With a true heart and in fulness of faith' further define the 'boldness' mentioned in v. 19.

*having our hearts sprinkled.* The participles are in the past tense, and are not, strictly speaking, so much a part of the exhortation as the ground on which it is based. 'Let us draw near, for we have had our hearts sprinkled . . . and our bodies washed.' (We have been converted and baptized.) The author has so chosen his words as to suggest the priesthood of all Christians (cf. 1 Peter 2⁹, Rev. 1⁶), an idea which is, indeed, implied in the exhortation 'to enter into the holy place' (v. 19). Lev. 8³⁰ relates that Moses 'took of the blood which was upon the altar and sprinkled it upon Aaron . . . and upon his sons', thus 'sanctifying' them to their priestly office. Exod. 29⁴ enacts washing with water as a feature in the ceremonial of the consecration of a Jewish priest.

23. The opening words (cf. 4¹⁴) go well with the reference to Baptism which immediately precedes them. The 'confession of hope' was first made at Baptism. The verse is thus a reminder of baptismal vows (cf. 1 Tim. 6¹²).

*he is faithful that promised.* The question 'will you be faithful to your baptismal promises, as God is to His promises?' is implied. Cf. the words in the Baptismal Office of the English Church, 'which promise He, for His part, will most surely keep and perform'.

24. *let us consider one another.* Compare the use of the same Greek word (κατανοεῖν) in 3¹. It does not mean 'let us be considerate to one another' but 'let us meditate upon one another'. Its meaning is represented exactly by Phil. 2⁴, 'not looking each of you to his own things, but each of you also to the things of others.'

*to provoke,* or, more exactly, 'as an incentive'. The Greek word (παροξυσμός from which our English 'paroxysm' is directly derived) is a very strong one. The whole idea is bold. Lack of charity is largely due to thoughtlessness. A little thought about their neighbour's rights and claims and needs will release in the hearts of Christians a full stream of practical lovingkindness. This, rather than competition in good works (an unpleasant idea), is probably the writer's meaning.

*good works.* The Greek word used is καλός (not ἀγαθός), with the characteristically Greek idea of the comeliness or attractiveness of what is good, the 'beauty of holiness' in contrast to the repulsiveness of evil, indicated in this Epistle by the phrase '*dead* works' (6¹, 9¹⁴).

25. An individualistic type of religion is anathema to the author, for whom Christianity is as essentially social as Judaism. The ideals of v. 24 are, he would say, incapable of realization if the practice of meeting together for mutual encouragement is neglected. Later Gnostics displayed a contempt for 'ordinary churchmen' and their practices. The 'enlightened' did not need to 'assemble themselves together'.

*ye see the day drawing nigh.* 'The day of the Lord' foretold by the Old Testament prophets (e.g. Amos 5¹⁸⁻²⁰) and the theme of the apocalyptists. One of the scanty, isolated fragments of conventional eschatology in the Epistle. See Introd., pp. 43 ff.

The characteristics of 'the day' are to some extent indicated in v. 27 and in 12²⁶ ᶠ.

## 10²⁶⁻³¹. *The fearfulness of apostasy.*

26. Gives the reason of the need of mutual exhortation, referred to in the previous verse.

For *wilfully*, as opposed to 'unconsciously', see Introd., pp. 46 f.

*there remaineth no more a sacrifice for sins.* This is in accordance with the strict Jewish theory of sacrifices, which were not held to avail for 'willing' sin. See Introd., pp. 45 f. The way in which the statement is worded is due to what has gone before in the argument. The Jewish sacrifices were futile. Christ's sacrifice cannot be repeated. Therefore there is no sacrifice 'left over'. (Gr. ἀπολείπεται: cf. καταλειπομένης in 4¹ and ἀπολείπεται in 4⁶ and 4⁹, with notes *ad loc.*)

27. The verse is connected in thought with the 'approaching day', cf. v. 25. Its language is borrowed from the LXX of Isa. 26¹¹. Cf. 12²⁹.

28. With the *a fortiori* argument, which begins in this verse, cf. 2² ᶠ. The reference in the 'Law of Moses' is Deut. 17²⁻⁶, where the offence contemplated is apostasy. See, further, Introd., p. 47.

29. *the blood of the covenant.* See Introd., pp. 39 f.

*done despite.* Notice the tendency (not fully and consistently developed in the N.T. as a whole) to personify the Spirit.

30. *we know who it is that said.* The quotation follows in the same form as in Rom. 12¹⁹, differing from any extant version of Deut. 32³⁵. Is this due to direct influence of St. Paul on the writer? Or are both

drawing from a Greek version no longer extant? The former supposition is possible. See the influence of Romans on Hebrews indicated in Introd., p. 16. But the second quotation in this verse comes from Deut. 32³⁶ (not quoted in Rom. 12¹⁹), a fact which suggests that the writer is here borrowing directly from Deuteronomy and not from St. Paul.

**31.** Cf. 2 Sam. 24¹⁴.

The author uses the phrase 'living God' to suggest fear in 3¹² and in the present verse, hope in 9¹⁴ and 12²².

*10³²⁻³⁷. Fall not at the eleventh hour from your former faith.*

**32-9.** The theme of this section is (in the words of v. 23) 'let us hold fast the confession of our hope'.

**32.** It would be deplorable to fall now below your own high standard. Realize that you have a great tradition to maintain, a noble record in the past, in times and circumstances no less difficult than the present.

*enlightened.* Cf. 6⁴ and note *ad loc*. Here it suggests the fresh brightness of their early faith.

**33.** *partly.* More exactly, 'on the one hand . . . on the other hand'.

*being made a gazingstock.* 'Being made *a spectacle*' gives the exact sense of the Greek word (θεατριζόμενοι); cf. 1 Cor. 4⁹.

*by reproaches and afflictions.* Their sufferings had gone beyond unpopularity and abuse to a certain measure of persecution, viz. the spoiling of their possessions (v. 34).

*and becoming partakers with* (Gr. κοινωνοί. A less vague word than the author's usual μέτοχος. Cf. the use of the noun (κοινωνία) in 13¹⁶.) Having no historical records of the events to which the writer is alluding we cannot with certainty appreciate the subtle difference between two kinds of experience indicated in this and the following verse. While the members of the church to whom the Epistle was addressed had themselves only suffered abuse and the spoiling of their goods, they had shown active sympathy with certain others (their Christian teachers, perhaps, see 13⁷ and note, or the members of a neighbouring church) with whom persecution had gone further and taken the form of actual imprisonment. So much is clear.

**34.** The position of 'yourselves' in the Greek is so emphatic that we must translate 'knowing that ye have *yourselves,* which is a better and abiding possession': indeed the whole passage is strongly reminiscent of Luke 21¹⁹ 'in your patience ye shall possess your souls'. In further support of the above translation of the present verse see note on v. 39.

*and abiding.* We are drawing near to the great chapter (11) which describes the 'abiding' City. The contrast between what is transient and what is abiding or eternal is characteristic of the whole Epistle. For a summary of this leading idea see 12²⁶, ²⁷.

35. 'It would be madness to cast aside this boldness now, for' (as the following verses proceed to suggest) 'it is now the eleventh hour.'

*recompense of reward.* For the use of this word in Hebrews see Introd., p. 49. Boldness will be rewarded because of the nature of God (11⁶), who richly rewards them that seek Him out.

36. Patience is all that is needed now. 'Through patience receiving the promise' (cf. 6¹²) is the theme of the great chapter which follows.

37. The quotations (from Isa. 26²⁰ and Hab. 2³) suggest 'the Day drawing nigh' (v. 25). It is the eleventh hour.

### 10³⁸–11⁴⁰. *What faith is and what it can achieve.*

38. In the meantime 'the righteous shall live by faith'. The quotation is from Hab. 2⁴, the verse following that quoted in v. 37.
We must take this verse as the introduction to the magnificent oration on faith which follows in chap. 11. Note how it is echoed in 11⁴ (Abel 'by faith *righteous*'), 11⁷ ('Noah by faith heir of the righteousness which is according to faith'), 11³³ ('through faith wrought righteousness'). In fact 'the righteous shall live by faith' is the text of the sermon which is now to follow.

39. The point of these verses is to make the readers feel at the outset that they are enrolled in the great company of the faithful which the author is about to display before their eyes. He postulates the same close affinity between his readers and the faithful departed at the end of the oration on faith (in 11⁴⁰), as he now emphasizes at its beginning.

39. *saving of the soul.* The Greek word (περιποίησιν) should be translated, as in 1 Pet. 2⁹, 'possession'. 'We are of faith unto the possessing of the soul', an echo of the language of v. 34 (see note).

11. 1. We begin the great chapter with the famous definition of faith—as 'sure confidence of things hoped for, conviction of things not seen'. Such a translation is more correct than the more metaphysical rendering in the A.V. There is nothing intellectualistic in

the writer's conception of faith. As he illustrates it in the succeeding verses, it is a frame of mind, an attitude towards life, which greets things hoped for as the certainties of the future, and embraces the unseen spiritual things as being alone the real.

*assurance.* The author has already used the word (ὑπόστασις) in the sense of 'sure confidence' in 3^{14} (see note *ad loc.*).

*proving* (ἔλεγχος): 'conviction' is better, for faith is not so much a process of proving as a conviction, similar to the outcome of proof.

We shall see in the course of the chapter how this general definition of faith is illustrated by the particular instances enumerated.

2. *the elders* is here not a technical title of an official class, but a general description of the people of past ages, our predecessors, as in the phrase 'the tradition of the elders'. Cf. 'the fathers' in 1^1.

*had witness borne to them,* i.e. in the pages of the sacred writings. Note the repetition of the phrase in vv. 4 f.; and compare 7^{8, 17} and 10^{15}.

3. The writer has, so to speak, opened his Old Testament to expound from beginning to end the achievements of faith, and his eye rests on Gen. 1.

The verse is a general statement, as against materialism, of the idealist position. It is more than the affirmation of belief in creation *ex nihilo*. *It is the assertion of faith that 'things unseen' are the ultimately real.*

*out of things which do appear.* The Universe is not a matter of mere phenomena. There is spiritual meaning and purpose behind it. The author would have subscribed heartily to Rom. 1^{20}, with which the present verse has close affinity.

4. Why was Abel's sacrifice acceptable and Cain's rejected? The author of Hebrews boldly declares that it was because Abel had faith, which Cain lacked; an inference which he draws simply from the fact that God accepted Abel's offering. ('God bearing witness in respect of his offering'; for, as he remarks in v. 6, without faith it is impossible to be well pleasing to God.)

*and through faith he being dead yet speaketh.* The phrasing is determined by Gen. 4^{10}, 'the voice of thy brother's blood crieth unto me from the ground'. See 12^{24}. But the writer means that faithful Abel has a message for his readers. Philo writes similarly about Abel, as living though he seemed to be dead. (*Quod det. potiori insid. soleat*, 14 and 20.)

5. The writer infers Enoch's faith from his translation, and from Gen. 5²⁴, where the LXX 'witnesses' that Enoch 'pleased God'; in place of the statement in the Hebrew version that Enoch 'walked with God'.

6. Rather naïvely, the author remarks that Enoch must have

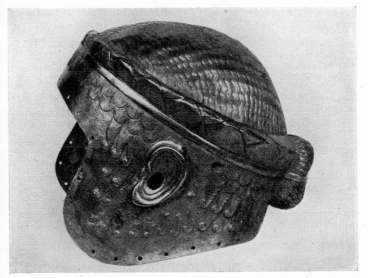

The magnificent civilization of Ur. The gold helmet or headdress of a Sumerian prince, dating from the third millennium B.C.

had faith, for otherwise he could not have pleased God. He then attempts to prove his statement. You cannot, he implies, please God without 'coming unto' Him (προσερχόμενον 'drawing near in worship', once again), and you cannot, he says, worship without faith. Therefore Enoch had faith. Faith, in this context, consists in belief in the reality of God ('conviction of things not seen') and in His readiness to reward the search of those who seek Him out ('assurance of things hoped for').

7. Noah's faith in providing against the Flood is explicitly

defined as 'conviction of things not seen'. The Flood was not seen as yet when Noah prepared the Ark.

*moved with godly fear.* Cf. the same word in 5[7] and 12[28].

*through which,* i.e. through his faith; cf. 'through it' in v. 4.

*he condemned the world.* This is a strange statement of the achievement of Noah's faith. Presumably Noah 'condemned the world' by assenting to God's pronouncement that the Flood would come to punish the wickedness of the human race. His faith responded to the divine sentence of condemnation.

*became heir.* Such was the status of those under the Old Covenant who had faith. They received not the promises (v. 13), but became enrolled as qualified to inherit them, when the time should come for their realization. Cf. vv. 39–40, and see note on 9[15].

*of the righteousness which is according to faith.* The phrase has a Pauline tone, but in the context is a direct reference back to 10[38], which as we have seen is the 'text' of the present chapter.

8. The faith of Abraham is so described in these verses as to fall clearly under the definition of v. 1. The venture of Abraham to which this verse refers has been heightened by the traces of a magnificent civilization recently excavated in Ur of the Chaldees (Gen. 11[31]).

9. *of the same promise,* i.e. primarily the promise of possession of the land of Canaan, one of those temporary promises which those of the Old Covenant in due time 'obtained' (v. 33); but, as in 6[13-18] (see notes on 6[17 f.]), the writer would not exclude the ultimate Messianic significance of the promise to Abraham, the promises which those of the Old Covenant saw only from afar (v. 13).

10. *city which hath the foundations,* a securely founded city, in contrast to the 'moving tents' of the preceding verse. See further Introd., p. 29.

11. *even Sarah,* who was past child-bearing, and who at first doubted.

*counted him faithful who had promised.* Cf. 10[23]. The promise in this case is, of course, the birth of Isaac.

12. Note the attractive manner in which the author in these verses represents the birth of Isaac, as being achieved by the combined faith of Abraham and Sarah.

*him as good as dead.* Cf. Rom. 4[19]. St. Paul, rather characteristically, ignores the faith of Sarah.

13. With the wisdom and skill of a literary or rhetorical artist

the writer redeems his historical survey from all danger of monotony by the interpolation of these verses, 13–16.

*the promises.* They realized promises (v. 33) but not 'the promises'. Beyond their temporary achievements the hope of yet greater things spread onward into the future. Isaac was born, but Abraham and Sarah did not live to see their seed a universal blessing to all the earth (Gen. 22$^{18}$). (See notes on 6$^{17\,f.}$) Thus they were to the day of their death like pilgrims, their hope set on promises too great for realization within the small compass of a human lifetime. Of all faithful life the history of the nomadic patriarchs, dwelling in tents in expectation of a promise yet to be realized, is for the writer of the Epistle symbolic.

*confessed that they were strangers,* e.g. Gen. 23$^4$, 47$^9$.

14. *they that say such things . . .* Men who use such language as that quoted in the previous verse clearly imply that they are seeking a fatherland. They would not realize that they were strangers and pilgrims here, unless they were conscious of belonging elsewhere.

15. It was not of Mesopotamia, from which they had come, that they were thinking when they confessed themselves strangers in Palestine. They could have returned thither, but they did not.

16. Clearly therefore the fatherland which they desired must be a heavenly.

*God is not ashamed.* Cf. 2$^{11}$. A bolder and rather more attractive way of saying God deigns or condescends. God goes out to meet the faith of the patriarchs, because He is 'rewarder of them that seek Him out' (v. 6).

*to be called their God.* The reference is to the phrase constantly recurring in the O.T. 'I am the God of Abraham, and the God of Isaac, and the God of Jacob.'

17–18. The supreme example of Abraham's faith. He had staked everything on the promises. They were to be realized through Isaac his son. None the less he was prepared to sacrifice Isaac at God's command. In fact, as the imperfect tense implies, he was in the very act of offering him up.

19. In obeying the command to sacrifice Isaac he did not surrender his faith in the promise of all that was to come through Isaac.

*in a parable.* There are two possible meanings, either, simply,
'metaphorically speaking'; or the author means that Abraham
achieved, so to speak, a parable or 'type' of the restoration of the
sacrificed Christ from the dead. For 'parable' in the sense of 'type'
see 9⁹.

20. Isaac's assurance of things hoped for, his conviction of
things not seen.

21. These illustrations of faith are drawn from the closing
hours of the patriarchs and thus reinforce the words of v. 13 that
they *died* in faith, that to the very end they cherished the assurance of things hoped for, confessing that here they were strangers
and sojourners with no abiding city, seeking one to come (13¹⁴).

*worshipped, leaning upon the top of his staff.* So the LXX of Gen.
47³¹. The Hebrew has, instead of 'staff', 'bed'.

The words of this verse are intended to heighten the effect of the
picture of the faith in which Jacob died. They are taken from
a different context from the blessing of Joseph's sons, viz. Jacob's
instruction that he should be buried outside Egypt in the burying-
place of his fathers in the Promised Land. They suggest therefore
yet another instance of Jacob's faith.

22. So confident was Joseph of things hoped for, promised but
not seen, viz. the Exodus.

23. The faith of Moses' parents, stronger than fear.

24–25. The faith of Moses, rising superior to material prosperity
and worldly ambition.

25. *the pleasures of sin.* This unfavourable description of Egyptian
civilization is not surprising in view of the record of the cruel
Egyptian oppression of the people of God.

*for a season*, in contrast to the eternal nature of the ideal to
which he responded.

26. *the reproach of Christ*, more exactly, 'the reproach of the
Messiah', cf. 13¹³. Westcott (*Commentary*, p. 374) calls attention
to Ps. 89⁵⁰ ᶠ·, 'the reproach . . . wherewith they have reproached
the footsteps of thine anointed (Heb. Messiah)'. The reproach of
folly is often levelled by the world at those who sacrifice comfort
and advancement as did Moses and a Greater than Moses. Cf.
'fools for Christ's sake' in 1 Cor. 4¹⁰.

*for he looked.* Gr. ἀπέβλεπεν='he looked away'. Moses' faith
looked away from the visible riches to the 'unseen' recompense of
reward. Cf. 'he endured as seeing him who is invisible' in the
following verse; and 12² with note.

*recompense of reward.* (Cf. $2^2$, $10^{35}$.) Re-echoes faith's conviction that God 'is a rewarder of them that seek Him out', expressed in $11^6$. The nature of the reward is defined in $10^{35,\ 39}$ (see notes) as the possessing of our own souls.

27. *not fearing the wrath of the king.* Is the reference to Moses' flight into the land of Midian? But this would be difficult to reconcile with Exod. $2^{15}$ which directly attributes Moses' flight to his fear of Pharaoh. More probably the reference is to the Exodus, in the course of achieving which Moses displayed great fearlessness of the King of Egypt.

27. *for he endured, as seeing him who is invisible,* i.e. by the faith which is conviction of things not seen. Moses was inspired by faith in a 'living God' who is a rewarder of them that seek Him out (v. 6), and the fear of whom (cf. $10^{31}$) drove out the fear of Pharaoh.

28. In this instance the faith of Moses is exactly parallel to that of Noah described in v. 7 (see note), viz. a conviction of things (in the one case the Flood, in the other the destruction of the first-born) 'not seen as yet'.

31. Rahab appears as an instance of justification by *works* in James $2^{25}$. In 2 Esdras $9^{7\ f.}$, $13^{23}$, &c., there are indications of the existence of a purely Jewish controversy about justification by faith or by works. Probably Abraham and Rahab and others were favourite instances adduced by the disputing rabbis on either side.

*with them that were disobedient.* In what sense were the inhabitants of Jericho disobedient? In Joshua $2^{9\cdot13}$ Rahab tells the spies that she and her fellow-townsmen have heard of all the wonders which God had wrought for the Israelites. She begs that she and her family may be spared when God gives Jericho into their hand. In not submitting themselves, after Rahab's example, to the people for whom God was so clearly working the inhabitants of Jericho were 'disobedient'. On the other hand Rahab's faith was conviction of 'things not seen', viz. the imminent fall of Jericho.

32. For the technical rhetorical turn of phrase see Introd., p. 15.

33. *obtained promises.* See the similar phrase in $6^{15}$, and notes on $6^{17\ f.}$ and $11^{13}$.

*stopped the mouths of lions.* Dan. $6^{22}$.

34. *quenched the power of fire.* Dan. $3^{25}$.

*armies of aliens*. The Greek word ($\pi\alpha\rho\epsilon\mu\beta o\lambda\acute{a}s$) means, more properly, 'camping place', and is so used in 13<sup>13</sup>. It is used, as here, of an army in 1 Macc., e.g. 3<sup>15</sup>, 'Of aliens' ($\dot{a}\lambda\lambda o\tau\rho\acute{\iota}\omega\nu$), also is found in 1 Macc., e.g. 2<sup>7</sup>. It is in fact, as will presently appear, primarily of the heroes and martyrs described in the Books of Maccabees that the author is thinking in the verses which immediately follow.

35. *Women received their dead.* The reference is not only to the widow of Zarephath (1 Kings 17) and the Shunammite (2 Kings 4), but to 2 Macc. 7, where we read of the mother of seven sons who were put to death by Antiochus Epiphanes. The mother's words in 2 Macc. 7<sup>29</sup> have influenced the wording of the present verse, 'Fear not this butcher but, proving thyself worthy of thy brethren, accept thy death, that in the mercy of God I may *receive thee again* with thy brethren.' If the reference is to this woman, then the reunion primarily intended is 'the better resurrection' (see the end of the verse) rather than any restoration to this life.

*others were tortured*. The Greek verb ($\dot{\epsilon}\tau\nu\mu\pi\alpha\nu\acute{\iota}\sigma\theta\eta\sigma\alpha\nu$) is formed from the noun 'tympanon', the word used to describe the instrument of torture on which Eleazar the scribe was martyred (2 Macc. 6<sup>19</sup>). It seems to have been a frame on which the victim was stretched to be beaten to death (see 2 Macc. 6<sup>30</sup>). Eleazar 'did not accept deliverance', refusing the swine's flesh, the eating of which would have secured his release.

*that they might obtain a better resurrection*—an assurance of things hoped for, a conviction of things not seen.

37. *they were tempted.* This assorts strangely with the descriptions of particular sufferings which surround it in the context. No less than five plausible emendations of the word ($\dot{\epsilon}\pi\epsilon\iota\rho\acute{a}\sigma\theta\eta\sigma\alpha\nu$) have been suggested. Of these the best is 'they were burned' ($\dot{\epsilon}\pi\nu\rho\acute{\omega}\theta\eta\sigma\alpha\nu$), as were some of the Maccabean martyrs (2 Macc. 6<sup>11</sup>, 7<sup>5</sup>).

38. *of whom the world was not worthy*, i.e. They belonged to a 'better country'. A parenthetical outburst.

*caves*. See 2 Macc. 6<sup>11</sup>.

39. *having had witness borne to them*. Better '*Although* they are chronicled in the pages of Scripture through their faith'. For this meaning of witness see 7<sup>17</sup>, 11<sup>2</sup> (and note), 11<sup>4 f.</sup>.

*received not the promises*. Cf. 11<sup>13</sup> (see note *ad loc*.). They obtained temporary promises (v. 33) but not *the* (Messianic) promises.

40. Suddenly and dramatically the full significance, for the readers of the epistle, of the pageant of the faithful of past ages is revealed. We have become engrossed in their history, lost in wonder at their heroism and in the beauty of the language in which it is described; and suddenly we are told in these concluding verses that we are in a more favourable position than was theirs on earth: for to us has been given in Christ the realization of all promises. The content of their faith was but an imperfect part of what we are now invited to enjoy. The thought gives almost a sinister significance to the picture of these heroes as an encompassing cloud of witnesses with which the following chapter opens. It burdens us with a heavy sense of our responsibility. vv. 39, 40 must be read in the light of 9¹⁵, see note.

Before leaving chapter 11 we should remark how completely this splendid record of the practical achievements of those who had faith lifts us above the level of the wretched controversies of 'faith' and 'works'.

### 12¹⁻¹³. *Helps in running the hard race.*

**12. 1.** *cloud.* The Greek word (νέφος) is similarly used by Herodotus (8. 109) for a host of men.

*of witnesses.* The word is an echo of the frequent 'those who had witness borne to them' of chapter 11. But it is no longer in the passive but the active voice. The thought is of the witness which the faithful bore to God, to the better fatherland, to the city having foundations. It does not mean 'spectator'. Nevertheless, the writer conceives of the cloud of witnesses looking on at the race which we are running. So much is unmistakably implied in the cloud 'compassing about' the course. The heroes of old watch our race; we, in the running of it, look to Christ (v. 2).

*weight* is, literally, too heavy a translation. The Greek word (ὄγκος) is used of the minor encumbrances such as clothing, or superfluous flesh of which the athlete divests himself. The more serious encumbrances to Christian running are referred to in the words that follow. Here the reference is to the little things without which, though not seriously harmful in themselves, we should run better.

*which doth so easily beset us.* The marginal translation 'is admired of many' has serious claims for consideration. The Greek word (εὐπερίστατον), which is not found elsewhere, would most naturally mean 'well-befriended', i.e. 'greatly admired'. 'The sin admired by the world is worse than useless if life is a contest' (perhaps with a secondary thought that it is not admired by the encompassing cloud of witnesses).

In any case 'which doth so easily beset' does not give the sense of the word. The only possible alternative to 'greatly-admired' is 'well placed around', i.e. thoroughly encumbering, like a thick encompassing garment which completely hampers the runner or overthrows him.

2. *looking unto*. As in 11$^{26}$ (see note), 'looking away', i.e. from what is visible, to the unseen. With the whole of this line of thought, summarized in the word ἀφορῶντες, cf. 2 Cor. 4$^{18}$.

*author*. The same word ἀρχηγός as in 2$^{10}$ (see note). 'Jesus the Pioneer and Perfecter of Faith.' He both leads the way and perfects the process; for from Him come both the example and the power to follow it.

*who for the joy*. Such an example of patience and faith, such an assurance of victory through endurance is exactly what the readers of the Epistle needed.

3. Therefore 'consider Him'. 'He like you had to endure the *gainsaying of sinners*.' His persecution is described in this general way, because the analogy which the author is trying to establish between Christ and his readers demanded a certain vagueness, inasmuch as they had 'not yet resisted unto blood'.

*sinners against themselves*. Cf. Num. 16$^{38}$. If the marginal reading, which is well supported, be correct, 'against himself' goes with 'gainsaying' and not with 'sinners'.

4. You have not yet been called upon to suffer as He suffered.

*Sin*. Persecution is always in some degree the outcome of the essential antagonism between goodness and sin.

5. It is possible to take this verse interrogatively. 'Have ye forgotten?'

The quotation from Prov. 3$^{11 f.}$ is a warning against two distinct wrong reactions to suffering. (1) It is wrong to take it lightly, with stoical indifference, failing to learn from it. (2) It is wrong to faint because of it, to lose faith and hope.

6. Suffering has its significance, viz. the discipline which love provides for those whom it would lead to maturity of will and mind and heart.

7. *chastening* (παιδείαν). It is important that this word should here be rendered 'education'. 'It is for education that ye endure.' Education (as the quotation from Proverbs implies) is the purpose of discipline. *Paideia* means all the discipline of education.

8. Discipline is an essential part of the relation of father and son. Cf. the idea underlying 2¹⁰.

9. *and live.* The author appeals to his readers' sense of the value of the discipline provided by the 'fathers of their flesh'. Much more might they expect fullness of life as the outcome of a reverent, teachable reaction to the discipline of the 'Father of spirits'.

10. For human fathers with a merely temporal end in view chastened us sometimes arbitrarily but, at the best, according to the dictates of their fallible judgement. With Him you may be sure that chastening is always wisely directed to our profit, and to no transient end but to make us partakers of His eternal nature.

Discipline, as has been said above, is an essential part of the relationship of father and son, and sons are 'partakers of' their father's nature.

*holiness.* The root meaning of the Hebrew word for 'holy' is 'separate'. Earthly suffering which (if rightly accepted) detaches the affections from earthly things makes us partakers of the divine separateness. Cf. 'separated from among sinners' in 7²⁶.

11. *unto them that have been exercised thereby.* A very important part of the sentence. Not every sufferer attains to peace and righteousness through suffering, not those, for instance, who fall under either of the categories suggested in v. 5 (see note *ad loc.*). Cf. 'exercised' in 5¹⁴. In the present verse it means 'those who have by practice acquired the capacity of reacting rightly to affliction'.

12. For this verse the writer is indebted to Isa. 35³.

*wherefore.* Take courage because though affliction is bound to be painful it is within your power to make its outcome righteousness and peace.

13. *make straight paths for your feet.* Cf. Prov. 4²⁶. It is possible to translate 'make straight paths with your feet'. This rendering suits better the words which follow. 'If the community as a whole walks firmly straight ahead, the weaker brethren, the stragglers, will the more easily follow.'

*be not turned out of the way.* The marginal translation 'be not put out of joint' is certainly correct. The Greek word ($\dot{\epsilon}\kappa\tau\rho\alpha\pi\hat{\eta}$) is the technical term for the dislocating of a joint. 'But rather be healed' then follows naturally.

12^{14-17}. *Your sanctification must not be compromised.*

14. *Follow after peace with all men.* Ps. 34^{14}. More than a mere desire for peace is enjoined, but a willingness to go to some distance to secure it.

*with all men.* With those outside the Church as well as with those within.

*and the sanctification.* A warning is implied, setting limits to the pursuit of peace. You must not go so far as to compromise your sanctification.

*see the Lord.* Reminds us, in its context, of 'Blessed are the pure in heart for they shall *see God*'.

15. Arises from fear of the possibility of their losing their sanctification. It is dangerous for the community to harbour even a single corrupt member.

*any root of bitterness.* The expression comes from Deut. 29^{18}. The translation is unfortunate as suggesting that contentiousness was the evil influence which the writer feared. 'Root of bitterness' is a characteristic Hebraism for 'bitter root'; and the meaning is a poisonous growth which spreads decay around it. The reference in Deut. 29^{18} is to apostasy issuing in moral corruptness. For the moral corruptness in the present context see the next verse.

16. *fornicator.* See Introd., p. 47.

*profane person, as Esau.* Profane because he thinks so lightly of spiritual issues that he sets his bodily appetites higher in the scale of values.

17. The rigorism of the author again (see Introd., pp. 45 ff.). He is in part influenced here by the stern words which follow, in Deut. 29^{18-20}, upon the reference to 'the root that beareth gall and wormwood' (see Introd., p. 47).

The relevant passages in Esau's history will be found in Gen. 25^{33 f.}, 27^{30-40}. The author of Hebrews characteristically reads into the words of Genesis more than is explicit in them. He represents Jacob's acquisition of the blessing which should have been Esau's as due to Esau's sale of the birthright to Jacob. Actually the two stories are two alternative versions (from E. and J. respectively) of the supplanting of Esau by Jacob.

*place of repentance.* The phrase occurs in Wisd. 12^{10}.

Esau's *tears*, as Moffatt remarks, are not mentioned in the particular text of the LXX (the A text) which the author seems generally to have used. But they are found in the other texts of the LXX and in Jubilees 26^{33}.

## 12<sup>18-29</sup>. *Sinai and Zion.*

18. *For ye are not come.* Again the author's favourite word (προσεληλύθατε) 'to draw near in worship'. Your sanctuary is not Sinai but Zion, the real Holy Place in the heavens. The connexion with what goes before may be thus indicated. 'You have need to look carefully because of the greatness of your privileges. In Christ you have been brought into the innermost sanctuary of God.'

The whole paragraph is a final contrast of the inferiority of the Old Covenant promulgated on Sinai to the New Covenant.

*a mount that might be touched.* It is doubtful (see marginal rendering) whether the word 'mount' is to be supplied with 'tangible', whether 'tangible' is to be taken with fire, or whether the meaning is simply 'ye are not come unto a tangible (i.e. material) thing'.

In any case 'tangible' is in contrast to 'heavenly' in v. 22.

In vv. 18–21 words are piled up to suggest dramatically the confusion and fear which prevailed on Sinai.

*burned with fire . . . and darkness.* See Deut. 4<sup>11</sup>.
*tempest, and the sound of a trumpet.* See Exod. 20<sup>18</sup>.
19. *the voice of words.* See Deut. 4<sup>12</sup>.
*which they had heard intreated . . .* See Deut. 5<sup>23-25</sup>.

20. *they could not endure that which was enjoined.* Then follows one of the utterances 'too terrible to be endured', viz. 'If even a beast . . .' (a free quotation from Exod. 19<sup>12 f.</sup>).

We must beware of reading into this verse the Pauline idea that the Law of Sinai was too hard to be kept. The instance given of a commandment which could not be endured shows the meaning, viz. that the utterances of the voice, because of the awful unapproachableness which they suggested, were too terrible to be borne. (Keeping beasts and people back from Mt. Sinai would not be a suitable illustration of a law too hard to fulfil!)

21. *the appearance* (Gr. τὸ φανταζόμενον). Better 'the apparition': cf. the use of the cognate substantive in Mark 6<sup>49</sup>, 'They thought that it was an apparition'.

*Moses said.* The writer misquotes from memory (cf. notes on 9<sup>19, 20, 21</sup>). Moses uttered words like these not about the terrors of Sinai but the abomination of the golden calf (Deut. 9<sup>19</sup>).

22. Notice the impressive transition from the atmosphere of chaos and terror around Sinai to the peace and confidence of 'Zion'.

*Zion.* This other 'mount' is the symbol of true worship. 'Ye are come' (i.e. in worship. See note on v. 18) 'to Zion.'

*the city of the living God.* Cf. 11¹⁰, ¹⁶, 13¹⁴. This idea of the heavenly Jerusalem, the archetype of the earthly, frequently appears in the recorded teaching of the rabbis. In the New Testament it is found also in Rev. 3¹², 21² ᶠᶠ· and in Gal. 4²⁶ ᶠ·

The Galatians passage offers a remarkable parallel to the present paragraph of Hebrews, inasmuch as the same contrast is presented between Mt. Sinai and the heavenly Jerusalem, though it is worked out on entirely different lines.

23. *to the general assembly.* These words should be taken with 'myriads of angels'. The Greek word (πανηγύρει) is used by Thucydides (e.g. i. 25) of the inhabitants of a Greek state assembled to celebrate the festival of their national games; and it appears occasionally in the sense of religious 'feast' or 'festival' in the LXX. 'To myriads of angels in festal assembly.'

*church of the firstborn,* i.e. the 'heirs' of whom we have heard much in the Epistle. Cf. 'heir' and 'firstborn' in 1² and 1⁶ (with notes). The idea of the Church comes over into Christianity from 'the congregation' of the whole Jewish people, of which we read in the Pentateuch, and which had become a commonplace of Jewish thought.

*to God the Judge of all.* As Westcott (*Comm., ad loc.*) points out, the order of the Greek words demands a different translation—'to the God of all as Judge'. Note that in spite of the author's exhortation to 'boldness' (4¹⁶, 10¹⁹), in spite of his emphasis on the privileges of Christians, who may enter into the innermost sanctuary, in spite of the fact that in the present passage he is engaged in contrasting the awfulness of Sinai with the security of Zion, he does not eliminate from his conception of true religion the element of awe (cf. also e.g. 12²⁹). To have done so would indeed have been incompatible with his leading conception of religion as worship.

*the spirits of just men made perfect.* Rather 'righteous men'. The translation 'just men' obscures the important fact that the words refer us back to 10³⁸, and to the 'righteous' enumerated in chapter 11. We were told that 'apart from us' it was God's plan that 'they should not be made perfect' (11⁴⁰). But now that the new covenant has been instituted it has availed 'for the redemption of the transgressions which were under the first covenant' (9¹⁵) and the righteous of past ages, who looked for promises greater than the old imperfect Covenant could ever realize, have been 'made perfect', i.e. the process of their salvation has been completed (see Introd., p. 48, on meaning of 'perfection' in Hebrews).

24. *mediator*. Cf. 8⁶ with note.

*blood of sprinkling*. Not propitiatory blood sprinkled on the 'mercy seat', but sacrificial blood the sprinkling of which on the people made them parties to a covenant (see Introd., p. 39, and 9¹⁹ᶠ, and note), or, in other circumstances, consecrated them to priesthood (10²² and note).

*speaketh better than that of Abel*. A reference back to 11⁴. 'Abel's blood for vengeance pleaded to the skies . . .' It is better with the author of Hebrews to leave unuttered all that the blood of Jesus speaketh.

25. *if they escaped not*. Those who disobeyed were 'thrust through'.

*on earth*, i.e. speaking in the 'voice of words' on Sinai.

*him that warneth from heaven*, i.e. Him who utters the words quoted in v. 26. To reinforce the idea of a voice *from heaven* the writer chooses a text which proclaims the shaking of the heavens.

26. *shook the earth*. See Exod. 19¹⁸. Moffatt remarks that this earthquake does not appear in the text of the LXX (the A text) which our author seems to have used. See, however, Ps. 68⁸.

*Yet once more . . .* Quoted from Hag. 2⁶.

27. Shows why the author has described the quotation as a promise.

*signifieth the removing of those things that are shaken*. The writer interprets 'Yet once more' as meaning 'once for all'. 'Shaking' implies in the writer's mind material things. Such things were made, i.e. they had a beginning, and are not by nature eternal as are the spiritual things which are not subject to shaking. With these verses compare the words of the psalm quoted in 1¹¹ᶠ. For comment on the eschatology of these verses see Introd., pp. 43 ff.

28. An exhortation to thankfulness because the possessions of the Christian are not subject to shaking, and are beyond the reach of any catastrophe that may overtake the physical universe.

*that cannot be shaken*, because it is spiritual not material.

*let us have grace*. The marginal rendering 'let us have thankfulness' gives the straightforward meaning of the Greek words (ἔχωμεν χάριν), and is certainly to be preferred.

*we may offer service* (Gr. λατρεύωμεν). See Introd., p. 48. The technical term for taking part in worship in a sanctuary.

Thankfulness and godly fear alike the author declares to be essential elements in acceptable worship.

29. *for* (καὶ γάρ), 'for indeed' (Westcott). The verse gives the reason for the necessity of 'reverence and awe'. The words 'The Lord thy God is a devouring fire, a jealous God' occur in Deut. $4^{24}$ in the midst of the account of the theophany on Sinai (cf. Heb. $10^{27}$, 'jealousy of fire'; see margin).

### $13^{1-6}$. *Ethical precepts.*

**13.** 2. The importance of mutual hospitality as a virtue among the early Christians is a commonplace. In days when the inns were for the most part unsuitable lodging places for Christians, hospitality was essential to the extension of the Gospel and to intercommunion among the local churches.

*Forget not to shew love unto strangers: for thereby* . . . Cf. 'through it' (i.e. through faith) in $11^4$. For the moment the writer returns to the methods of chap. 11. Through hospitality some in the past have achieved the entertainment of angels. He is thinking of Abraham and Sarah (Gen. 18) and probably Tobit (Tobit $12^{15}$).

3. Sympathy is literally *feeling with*. 'As being yourselves also in *a* body you are therefore liable to the same afflictions and can feel with those who suffer them.' The verse throws light on the Christology of $2^{9-18}$, the Christ 'partaking of flesh and blood that he might become a merciful (or 'sympathetic') high priest'.

*body.* The word lacks the definite article. The above is therefore the correct interpretation. We are not at liberty to translate 'in the Body', and interpret by reference to 1 Cor. $12^{26}$.

4. All the emphasis is on 'honourable'. 'Honourable is marriage', or 'honourable let marriage be'. In view of the emphasis on 'honourable' it is possible that the author had in view not only those who depreciated marriage by immorality but those also who through a false asceticism, characteristic of a certain type of Gnostic, forbade marriage (1 Tim. $4^3$). See Introd., p. 23.

5. Note marginal rendering. 'Let your turn of mind be free from love of money.' 'Disposition' is a close equivalent to the Greek word (τρόπος).

The quotation which follows is not found exactly in this form in the LXX, though it is very like Joshua $1^5$. But Philo (*de Confus. Ling.* 32) gives the words in exactly the same form as in this verse.

6. Our response to the divine promise quoted in the preceding verse. The quotation in v. 6 is straight from the LXX of Ps. $118^6$.

$13^{7\text{-}9}$. *Remember your first Christian teachers and the faith
they held.*

7. *the issue.* The Greek (ἔκβασιν) means literally 'out-going'.
The hypothesis of a glorious martyrdom of their earliest teachers
and presbyters would give the words their fullest force. Perhaps
the wording of the sentence is deliberately vague, to include some
who had not been martyred but had none the less 'died in faith'
($11^{13}$).

8. Westcott is almost undoubtedly wrong in making this verse
begin a new paragraph. Moffatt has shown its close connexion
with the preceding verse. 'Human leaders may pass away, but
Jesus Christ, the supreme object and subject of their faithful
teaching, remains, and remains the same: no novel additions to
his truth are required' (Moffatt, *Comm.*, p. 231). Thus is verse 8
linked with what precedes and with what follows.

Cf. with this verse $7^{24\cdot 25}$.

9. For the importance of this verse, as indicating the nature
of the tendencies which the author was attempting to counteract,
see Introd., pp. 21 ff.

*It is good that the heart be established* . . . You must seek your
salvation in the sphere of spiritual influences not in that of outward rules and observances. How vain is the latter sphere witness
the whole of the preceding argument about the futility of the
Jewish sacrifices, 'wherein they that occupied themselves were
not profited'.

$13^{10\text{-}14}$. *Judaism is superseded and must be left behind.*

10. *We have an altar.* Not that we lack any good thing that was
represented by the outward cultus of Judaism. We have an altar
(cf. 'We have a High Priest', $8^1$). Controversy has raged around
this verse. To what is the author of Hebrews referring? Of one
thing we can be quite certain that he did not mean, by the 'altar',
the Cross of Christ. In his symbolism (see $13^{11\text{-}13}$ with notes) the
cross of Christ corresponds not with the altar where the blood of
the victim was offered, but with the place 'outside the camp',
where the victim's body was burned. 'Altar' in this verse is contrasted with 'tabernacle', and is thus part of the real sanctuary
in the heavens, which throughout the Epistle is contrasted with
its material copy, the Jewish Tabernacle. It is, then, the place
of Christ's offering whither He has passed with His blood (e.g.
$9^7$, $^{11\,f}$.), and to which we Christians have access ($10^{19}$). The

heavenly altar is the only interpretation congruent with the argument of the Epistle as a whole. By the words 'whereof they have no right to eat who serve the tabernacle' the author implies that Christians 'eat of' their altar, an idea which must imply, in the eyes of unprejudiced criticism, some reference to the Holy Communion. So clearly has the author the thought of 'eating of the altar' in his mind, that it would have seemed to him a legitimate and natural development to call the Holy Table at which Christians 'eat of' Him who was sacrificed for them, in a secondary sense, 'the altar'.

Nevertheless it should be noted that the parallelism of the ceremonial of the Day of Atonement fails a little at this point. (For another failure see note on 13¹¹.) For on the Day of Atonement the blood was offered *on the altar*, only 'to make atonement for the altar' (Lev. 16¹⁸). To make atonement for the people it was sprinkled not on the altar but on the mysterious 'mercy seat' (Lev. 16¹³⁻¹⁵). The 'altar' in Hebrews is, then, the equivalent in the world of spiritual realities to the mercy-seat of the Tabernacle. It is called 'Altar' and not mercy-seat inasmuch as of the sacrifices of the mercy-seat there was no eating; and in fact altar was the more normal symbol than mercy-seat for a place of offering. Cf. the way in which the author of Hebrews confuses the daily sacrifices of the altar with the annual sacrifice of the mercy-seat in 7²⁷ (see note).

*whereof they have no right to eat which serve the tabernacle.* 'Do not imagine you are missing anything through having no share in all that cultus. The truth is that you possess privileges and realities too great for those who stop short at the mere earthly copies of heavenly things.'

10–13. It is important to realize that the whole point of this passage lies in the exhortation with which it concludes in v. 13, 'Let us go forth unto him without the camp', i.e. 'let us make a clean and complete breach with Judaism'.

11. The parallel which the author attempts to draw is not quite exact. The animals on the Day of Atonement did not 'suffer outside the camp' for they were slaughtered within it. Lev. 16¹¹, ¹⁵. But Lev. 16²⁷ enacts that the bodies of the animals whose blood had been offered on the Day of Atonement were to be burned outside 'the camp', i.e. outside the area of the tents of 'the congregation' encamped around the Tabernacle.

12. Similarly Jesus suffered outside the gates of Jerusalem. This fact is implied in all the Gospels, but is explicit in John 19²⁰. Note how it has influenced the Matthean and Lucan versions of the parable of the husbandmen and the vineyard. Contrast Matt. 21³⁹ and Luke 20¹⁵ with Mark 12⁸.

*that he might sanctify* . . . See note on 10¹¹.

13. Our place therefore is outside the Jewish camp.

*bearing his reproach.* Cf. 11²⁶ (and note) and, in 12², 'the *shame* of the cross'. With the common tendency to mock at what is not understood Pagans and Jews alike reproached the early Christians with their lack of an elaborate cultus. They were reproached also for their refusal to identify themselves absolutely with any earthly polity, one of the explanations of Tacitus' famous charge that they were obsessed by 'hatred of the human race' (*Ann.* xv. 44). To the average pagan they presented an irritatingly baffling spectacle, being practically indistinguishable from the Jews, and yet appearing in separation from them, and to some extent in antagonism to them.

14. Connecting this verse with the reproach of Christ in v. 13, we may quote the words of the unknown writer of the Epistle to Diognetus. 'The Christians inhabit their own countries, but only as sojourners. . . . Every foreign country is a fatherland to them and every fatherland is a foreign country.' For possible references in these verses to the siege or fall of Jerusalem see Introd., pp. 29.

### 13¹⁵, ¹⁶. *The nature of the Christian cultus.*

15. The true nature of the Christian cultus.

*a sacrifice of praise.* Thus is the 'peace-offering' described in Lev. 7¹². Our sin-offering has been made, never to be repeated. The peace-offering, the sacrifice of thanksgiving, is left for us to make. We make it 'through Him', our High Priest.

*the fruit of lips.* This phrase, which suits so well the context of thanksgiving as an offering to God, is derived from Isa. 57¹⁹.

The sacrifices of a Christian, the author would say, are offerings of heartfelt thanksgivings for the great sacrifices of which he eats (v. 10).

16. Do not forget, he adds, those other legitimate, indeed necessary sacrifices of the Christian, viz. the offering of a good life and of deeds of lovingkindness to his brethren.

*to communicate.* The Greek (κοινωνία) appears again in 10^{33}. It is the outcome of the 'love of the brethren' for which the writer pleads in v. 1.

A better translation, perhaps, 'of well-doing and fellowship be not forgetful'.

## 13^{17-25}. *Concluding words.*

17. Notice the definite note of submission to authority especially necessary when heretical tendencies were abroad.

*for this were unprofitable for you.* Almost humorous. Certainly a situation in which their pastors were grieving for the loss of their souls would be 'unprofitable for them'.

18. *Pray for us.* We dare to ask it because 'we are persuaded that we have a good conscience . . .'

19. 'I specially want you to pray that God will quickly give me back to you.' Any kind of hindrance would account for these words, not necessarily the author's imprisonment, of which there is no other suggestion in the Epistle. In fact v. 23 (see note) suggests that the author will be visiting his readers almost immediately. It is for a safe and speedy voyage that in this verse he bids them pray.

20. Having asked for their prayers he at once makes a prayer for them. His prayer is reminiscent of the words of Isa. 63^{11} (LXX), 'Where is he that brought up out of the sea the shepherd of the sheep?'

This is the only explicit reference in the Epistle to Christ's Resurrection (6^2 is vague and general—'resurrection of dead persons'). The reason for the author's silence about the Resurrection is clear. He describes Christ's sacrifice in the imagery furnished by the ceremonial of the Day of Atonement when the high priest passed through the veil with the blood. He tends therefore to telescope together (if the expression is permissible) the death and ascension of Christ.

*the blood of the eternal covenant.* See Introd., p. 39.

21. *make you perfect* (Gr. καταρτίσαι). Literally, 'fit you out' or 'equip you in every good work unto the doing of his will'.

*to whom.* Probably to the God of Peace, though possibly to Christ.

22. *the word of exhortation.* We have seen how the purpose of even the most theological parts of the Epistle is essentially hortatory.

*in few words.* Many preachers in beginning announce that their words are to be few. Few have the temerity to claim it at the end.

But the writer wants to suggest the vastness and importance of his subject.

23. *set at liberty.* Moffatt (*Comm., ad loc.*) points out that the Greek word is used in Acts 28²⁵ in the sense of 'setting out'. The meaning may be simply 'Timothy has started on his way to you. If he is not delayed, I will wait until I can join him on his journey.'

24. This is a very politic verse, suggesting that the letter is primarily to the Christian laity. The writer would not presume thus to lecture their official teachers and rulers. See especially, 5¹².

*They of Italy.* See Introd., p. 27.

# INDEX

Advent, Second, 44 f., 84, **122** f.
Alexandria, 9, 11, 14, 17–20, 42, 94, 106 f.
Allegory, 18, 20.
Altar, 149 f.
Apollos, 10, 14 ff., 27.
Aquila, 12 f.
Aristides, 15.
Ascension, 87 f., 152.
Atonement, Day of, 32, 40, 44, 99, 110, 115, 117, 121, 123, 125, 150.

Baptism, **15**, 36, 102, 130.
Bate, Dean, 111.

Calvin, 9.
Cicero, 15.
Clement of Alexandria, 9.
Clement of Rome, 28.

Davidson, A. B., 45, 47, 97, 103.
Demosthenes, 15.
Diognetus, Epistle to, **151**.
Du Bose, 126.

Ecclesiasticus, **123**.
Ephesus, 27.
Epictetus, 101.
Esdras II, 84, 139.
Essenes, 22 f., 25 f., 86.
Eucharist, 120, 124, 150.
Eusebius, 9 f.

Gnosticism, 22–7, 30, 43, 46, 82, 86, 90, 109, 116, 122, 131, 148.

Harnack, 11 f.
Herodotus, 141.
Holy Ghost, 117, 131.
Homer, 18.

Intercession, Christ's, 36, **109**.
Isocrates, 15.
Italy, 15, 27.

Jerusalem, Fall of, 21, 29.
Josephus, 23, 25 f., 29, 86, 114, 121, 148.
Jubilees, Book of, 144.
Justin Martyr, 102.

Lightfoot, 22.
Logos, 20, 82, 84, 96.
Luther, 9, 14, 16.
LXX, 10, 26, 83, 84, 93, 95, 98, 120, 126, 131, 135, 138, 144, 146 f., 148, 152.

Melchizedek, 18, 27, 83, 100, 106 f.
Moffatt, 6, 15, 82, 92, 96, 108, 127, 144, 147, 149, 153.

Origen, 9 f.

Philo, 14, 17–20, 84, 87, 91 f., 96, 100 f., 104 f., 114, 134.
Pioneer, Christ as, 11, 31, 34, 49, 89.
Platonism, 17, 19, 26, 40, 42 f., 44, 48, 92, 112.
Priscilla, 10–13.

Quick, Canon, 42.

Resurrection, 88, **152**.
Rhetoric, 15, 49.
Rome, 27.

St. Barnabas, 10 f., 14, 20.
St. Bernard, 126.
St. Luke, 9–11, 129.
St. Paul, 9–12, 16, 22 f., 26, 95, 98, 101, 103 f., 118, 122 f., 125, 127 f., 131 f., 136, 145.
St. Peter, First Epistle of, 9, 12, 14, 101, 118, 129 f., 133.
Sanctification, 39 f., 127.
Scott, E. F., 15, 27, 81.
Silvanus, 10, 12.
Sophists, 18.
Sprinkling, 14, 39, **147**.

PRINTED IN
GREAT BRITAIN
AT THE
UNIVERSITY PRESS
OXFORD
BY
CHARLES BATEY
PRINTER
TO THE
UNIVERSITY

# THE CLARENDON BIBLE

## THE OLD TESTAMENT

Vol. I. THE HISTORY AND RELIGION OF ISRAEL.
By W. L. WARDLE.

Vol. II. FROM MOSES TO ELISHA: Israel to the end of the Ninth Century B.C. By L. ELLIOTT-BINNS.

Vol. III. THE DECLINE AND FALL OF THE HEBREW KING-DOMS: Israel in the Eighth and Seventh Centuries B.C. By T. H. ROBINSON.

Vol. IV. ISRAEL AFTER THE EXILE: Sixth and Fifth Centuries B.C. By W. F. LOFTHOUSE.

Vol. V. JUDAISM IN THE GREEK PERIOD: From the Rise of Alexander the Great to the Intervention of Rome (333 to 63 B.C.). By G. H. BOX.

Vol. VI. IN THE BEGINNING. An Introduction to the Early Hebrew Traditions of Genesis. By S. H. HOOKE.

## THE NEW TESTAMENT

ST. MATTHEW. By F. W. GREEN.

ST. MARK. By A. W. F. BLUNT.

ST. LUKE. By H. BALMFORTH.

THE ACTS OF THE APOSTLES. By A. W. F. BLUNT.

ROMANS. By K. E. KIRK.

CORINTHIANS. By E. EVANS.

GALATIANS. By A. W. F. BLUNT.

HEBREWS. By F. D. V. NARBOROUGH.

## THE SCHOOL CLARENDON BIBLE

Some volumes in the 'Clarendon Bible' are now being abridged and simplified for use in the middle form of schools and up to School Certificate standard.

ST. MATTHEW. By Miss B. K. RATTEY.

ST. MARK. By A. W. F. BLUNT.

ST. LUKE. By H. BALMFORTH.

ST. JOHN. By Miss B. K. RATTEY.

THE ACTS OF THE APOSTLES. By A. W. F. BLUNT.

ITALY

Rome
Three Taverns
Appii Forum
Puteoli

Rhegium

Syracuse

Melita

*SEA*

*OF*

*ADRIA*

MACEDONIA
Philippi
Neapolis
Amphipolis
Apollonia
Thessalonica
Beroea

GREECE
Athens
Corinth
Cenchreae

Phoenix
Cauda

Cyrene

Syrtis

The Near East i